DINOSAURS EYE TO EYE

Zoom in on the world's most incredible dinosaurs

LONDON, NEW YORK, MUNICH,
MELBOURNE, AND DELHI

Senior editor Shaila Brown
Senior art editor Philip Letsu
Art editor Johnny Pau
Managing editor Linda Esposito
Managing art editor Diane Thistlethwaite
Publishing manager Andrew Macintyre
Category publisher Laura Buller
Picture researcher Myriam Megharbi
DK picture library Emma Shepherd
Cartographer Ed Merrit
Creative technical support Peter Pawsey
Production editor Melissa Latorre
Production controller Charlotte Oliver
Jacket editor Joanna Pocock
Jacket designer Laura Brim
Jacket manager Sophia M Tampakopoulos Turner
Creative retouching Steve Willis

Consultant Dr Darren Naish

First published in Great Britain in 2010
This paperback edition published in 2013 by
Dorling Kindersley Limited, 80 Strand, London WC2R 0RL

Copyright © 2010 Dorling Kindersley Limited
A Penguin Company

2 4 6 8 10 9 7 5 3 1
194973 – 06/13

A CIP catalogue record for this book is
available from the British Library.

ISBN 978-1-4093-3403-3

Colour reproduction by MDP, United Kingdom
Printed by South China, China

Discover more at
www.dk.com

DINOSAURS EYE TO EYE

Zoom in on the world's most incredible dinosaurs

Author
John Woodward

Digital Sculptor
Peter Minister

Contents

6 Dinosaur timeline
8 What is a dinosaur?
10 Types of dinosaurs

12 **TRIASSIC WORLD**
14 Nothosaurus
16 Eoraptor
18 Coelophysis
20 Warm-blooded reptiles
22 Plateosaurus
24 Shonisaurus
26 Eudimorphodon
28 Isanosaurus

30 **JURASSIC WORLD**
32 Lesothosaurus
34 Rhomaleosaurus

36 Teeth and diet
38 Heterodontosaurus
40 Cryolophosaurus
42 Scelidosaurus
44 Barosaurus
46 Plates and spines
48 Stegosaurus
50 Allosaurus
52 Pterodactylus
54 Dinosaurs and birds
56 Archaeopteryx
58 Compsognathus

60 **CRETACEOUS WORLD**
62 Sauropelta
64 Deinonychus
66 Tenontosaurus

68 Spinosaurus
70 Scales and feathers
72 Citipati
74 Therizinosaurus
76 Crests and colours
78 Parasaurolophus
80 Triceratops
82 Pachycephalosaurus
84 Eggs and young
86 Saltasaurus
88 Quetzalcoatlus
90 Edmontosaurus
92 Tyrannosaurus

94 Glossary
96 Index
96 Credits

Fast Facts: the length or wingspan of each prehistoric animal is indicated in comparison to human dimensions – 1.8 m (6 ft).

What is a dinosaur?

We often think of dinosaurs as huge land-living reptiles that vanished off the face of the Earth many millions of years ago. Yet while some dinosaurs were certainly giants, others were relatively small, nimble creatures. One group even took to the air, and they still survive as birds. So our old image of dinosaurs as lumbering prehistoric monsters has changed dramatically. They were not like most of the cold-blooded reptiles we know today, but dynamic, probably warm-blooded creatures with distinctive anatomical features. The same could be said for the closely related pterosaurs that flew in the Mesozoic skies and evolved into the most spectacular flying animals of all time.

Reptiles with a difference
Dinosaurs were reptiles – part of a group that includes tortoises, crocodiles, and lizards. All these animals evolved from a shared ancestor that was almost certainly cold-blooded and scaly, like this lizard. But Mesozoic dinosaurs were probably warm-blooded, and many had feathers like modern birds. They were reptiles, but reptiles with a difference.

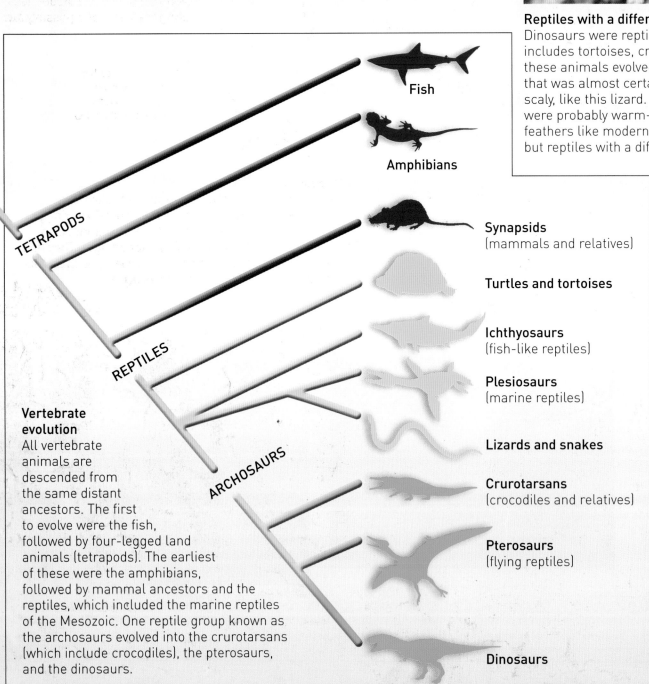

TETRAPODS

Fish

Amphibians

Synapsids
(mammals and relatives)

Turtles and tortoises

Ichthyosaurs
(fish-like reptiles)

REPTILES

Plesiosaurs
(marine reptiles)

Lizards and snakes

ARCHOSAURS

Crurotarsans
(crocodiles and relatives)

Pterosaurs
(flying reptiles)

Dinosaurs

Vertebrate evolution
All vertebrate animals are descended from the same distant ancestors. The first to evolve were the fish, followed by four-legged land animals (tetrapods). The earliest of these were the amphibians, followed by mammal ancestors and the reptiles, which included the marine reptiles of the Mesozoic. One reptile group known as the archosaurs evolved into the crurotarsans (which include crocodiles), the pterosaurs, and the dinosaurs.

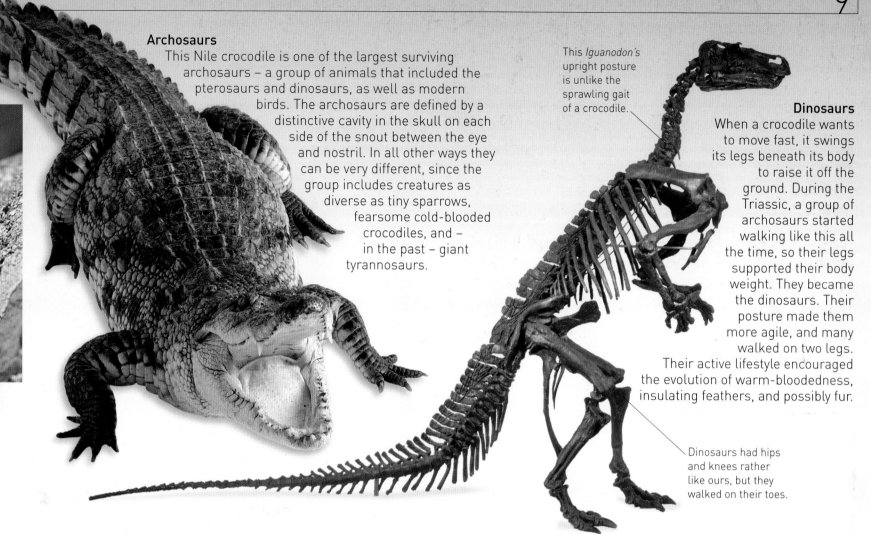

Archosaurs

This Nile crocodile is one of the largest surviving archosaurs – a group of animals that included the pterosaurs and dinosaurs, as well as modern birds. The archosaurs are defined by a distinctive cavity in the skull on each side of the snout between the eye and nostril. In all other ways they can be very different, since the group includes creatures as diverse as tiny sparrows, fearsome cold-blooded crocodiles, and – in the past – giant tyrannosaurs.

This *Iguanodon*'s upright posture is unlike the sprawling gait of a crocodile.

Dinosaurs

When a crocodile wants to move fast, it swings its legs beneath its body to raise it off the ground. During the Triassic, a group of archosaurs started walking like this all the time, so their legs supported their body weight. They became the dinosaurs. Their posture made them more agile, and many walked on two legs. Their active lifestyle encouraged the evolution of warm-bloodedness, insulating feathers, and possibly fur.

Dinosaurs had hips and knees rather like ours, but they walked on their toes.

Pterosaurs

One early group of archosaurs took to the air: the pterosaurs. They had furry bodies and bat-like wings made of skin reinforced with stiff fibres and muscles, supported by the bones of a single long finger. They had big flight muscles and flew well. But many, such as this *Pterodactylus*, also hunted on the ground.

Marine reptiles

Although they were not archosaurs and so not very closely related to dinosaurs, the Mesozoic marine reptiles were spectacular animals. Some, such as this *Mosasaurus*, were huge, powerful predators. Like the pterosaurs, they vanished at the end of the Mesozoic era.

Types of dinosaurs

Thousands of dinosaurs evolved during the Mesozoic era. We have found the remains of only a fraction of them, so scientists can never be sure that they have identified every main type. Yet the evidence shows that all dinosaurs except the earliest ones belonged to two groups – saurischians and ornithischians. These terms refer to the basic structure of their pelvic bones, but they were also distinguished by other features. For example, saurischians had longer, more flexible necks, and ornithischians had beaks supported by special jawbones. The saurischians evolved into the mainly meat-eating theropods and the plant-eating sauropodomorphs. The ornithischians split into three main types, nearly all plant-eaters.

Some sauropods had longer necks than any animals that have ever lived. The neck bones of *Brachiosaurus* were each up to 1 m (3 ft) long.

Sauropodomorphs

The sauropodomorphs included the biggest of all dinosaurs – huge sauropods like *Brachiosaurus*. They were all plant-eaters that needed big, heavy digestive systems. Their ancestors walked on their hind legs, but the giant sauropods supported their immense weight on four feet.

Family tree

This diagram shows the five main groups of dinosaurs. The theropods were mainly hunters such as the fearsome *Tyrannosaurus rex*. The sauropodomorphs included the huge, long-necked, plant-eating sauropods. The thyreophorans consisted of the stegosaurs and armoured ankylosaurs. These evolved before the ornithopods and marginocephalians, which included both horned ceratopsians and the pachycephalosaurs, or boneheads.

Saurischian dinosaurs had forward-pointing pubis bones in the pelvis. But later, some saurischians evolved their own version of the ornithischian-type pelvis.

All ornithischian dinosaurs had backward-pointing pubis bones in the pelvis. This allowed the heavy digestive system of a plant-eater to lie further back, so the animal's centre of gravity was nearer its hind legs.

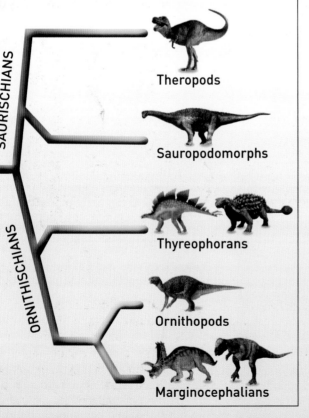

SAURISCHIANS

ORNITHISCHIANS

DINOSAURS

Theropods

Sauropodomorphs

Thyreophorans

Ornithopods

Marginocephalians

Many theropods had small front limbs, but those of tyrannosaurids were tiny.

Theropods

The theropods all walked on their hind legs, and nearly all of them were hunters. Some were powerful giants like this *Albertosaurus*. Others, such as *Velociraptor*, were smaller and more agile. Many had feathers, and one group of these that developed the ability to fly still survive – they are the birds.

Thyreophorans

In the Early Jurassic era, one branch of the ornithischian line evolved into the thyreophorans. There were two groups of these: stegosaurs like *Kentrosaurus* with its long spines and dorsal plates, and the heavily armoured ankylosaurs. The stegosaurs were mainly Jurassic, but ankylosaurs flourished during the Cretaceous.

Ornithopods

The ornithopods were one of the most successful groups of ornithischians. They were plant-eaters, like the sauropods, but their pelvic structure allowed their heavy intestines to lie further back in the body. This enabled many to walk upright, but bigger ones such as this *Iguanodon* often stood on four legs. They had chewing teeth, and like all ornithischians, they had short beaks.

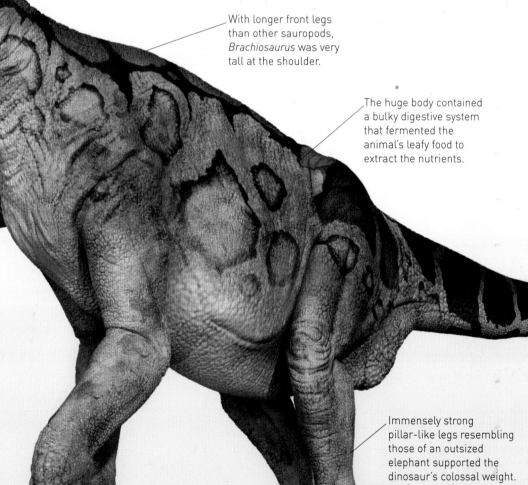

With longer front legs than other sauropods, *Brachiosaurus* was very tall at the shoulder.

The huge body contained a bulky digestive system that fermented the animal's leafy food to extract the nutrients.

Immensely strong pillar-like legs resembling those of an outsized elephant supported the dinosaur's colossal weight.

Marginocephalians

The last group of dinosaurs to appear were the marginocephalians. These included horned dinosaurs, or ceratopsians, like this *Einiosaurus*, and the pachycephalosaurs with their extra-thick "bonehead" skulls. The horns and frills of these animals were probably mainly ornamental.

Triassic world

The first dinosaurs appeared roughly halfway through the first period of the Mesozoic era – the Triassic, which lasted from 251 to 199 million years ago. The previous era – the Paleozoic – had ended in a catastrophic mass extinction that destroyed at least 90 per cent of all known living species. The surviving animals evolved into new forms that could take advantage of the conditions. Eventually, some 15 million years after the great extinction, this process gave rise to the dinosaurs. They took time to get into their stride, however, and did not start to dominate life on land until the Late Triassic, possibly because smaller extinction events had wiped out many of their competitors.

Supercontinent

The continents are in constant, very slow motion as they are carried around the globe by the mobile plates of the Earth's crust. In the Early Triassic, they had pushed together to form a supercontinent called Pangaea, surrounded by the Panthalassic Ocean. Pangaea started to break in two during the Late Triassic as the Tethys Ocean opened up.

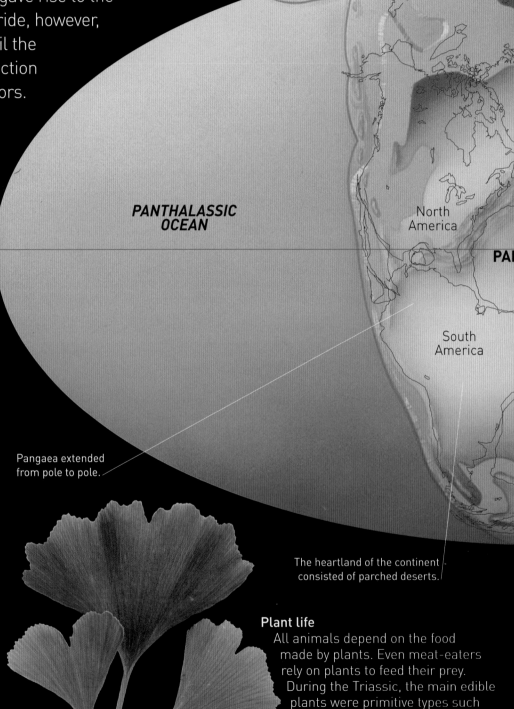

PANTHALASSIC
OCEAN

North
America

PAN

South
America

Pangaea extended
from pole to pole.

The heartland of the continent
consisted of parched deserts.

Climate

Large areas of land at the heart of Pangaea were a long way from the ocean. As a result, they got very little rainfall and were hot, arid deserts. Most of the plants and animals lived near the edges of the continent, where the influence of the ocean made the climate cooler and wetter.

Ginkgo
leaves

Plant life

All animals depend on the food made by plants. Even meat-eaters rely on plants to feed their prey. During the Triassic, the main edible plants were primitive types such as clubmosses, horsetails, and ferns, as well as conifer trees, ginkgos, and palm-like cycads. There were no grasses or flowering plants.

Insects and spiders

Although the mass extinction at the end of the Paleozoic destroyed a lot of animal life, many insects, spiders, and other invertebrates survived. They included creatures like this fossilized dragonfly. Over time, they flourished and evolved new forms, providing food for larger animals such as reptiles.

Thecodontosaurus was a primitive plant-eater.

Green and yellow indicate the area of land above sea level during the Triassic.

Siberia

Europe

North China

South China

Turkey

Indochina

Iran

GAEA

Tibet

Malaya

Africa   Arabia

TETHYS OCEAN

India

Australia

Antarctica

Red outline indicates how the Triassic continents split up to become today's continents or landmasses.

Dinosaurs

The dinosaurs evolved from a group of reptiles called the archosaurs, which also included a variety of crocodile-like creatures. The first dinosaurs were quite small compared to later ones, walked mainly on their hind legs, and ate a variety of foods. By the Late Triassic, such "all-purpose" dinosaurs, like this *Thecodontosaurus*, were evolving into more specialized hunters and plant-eaters.

Placerias

Mammal ancestors

For most of the Triassic, the dinosaurs were outnumbered by other animals such as lizards, tortoises, crocodilians, and mammal ancestors like *Placerias*. This hippo-like plant-eater was one of the last survivors of a group of animals that faded as the dinosaurs began to flourish – but not before giving rise to the first mammals.

Life in the water

Despite the mass extinction that ended the Paleozoic era, enough animals survived in the Triassic oceans to evolve into a wonderful variety of marine life. They included invertebrates, fish, and placodonts such as *Henodus* – an armoured reptile that fed mainly on shellfish.

The head was long and flat. It was rather like the head of a modern crocodile, primarily adapted for catching fish.

Nothosaurus had a long, flexible, well-muscled neck. This enabled it to throw its head sideways in the water to seize passing fish in its long jaws. This specialized "snap feeding" technique is used today by some crocodiles.

Nothosaurus

In the Middle Triassic, when the dinosaurs were just beginning to appear on land, the main oceanic fish hunters were nothosaurs like *Nothosaurus*. They were relatives of the plesiosaurs, but less aquatic. *Nothosaurus* fossils occur on sites that were once the northern shores of the ancient Tethys Ocean, where the animals probably hunted in shallow coastal waters.

Astonishingly long, sharp, interlocking teeth at the front of the jaws would have acted like skewers, impaling fish so that they had no chance of escape. With a quick flip of its head, *Nothosaurus* would have tossed them to the back of its mouth and swallowed them.

The animal almost certainly used its long, muscular tail to drive itself through the water, because its limbs were not highly adapted for swimming. Its tail improved its streamlining underwater and also accounted for much of the length of *Nothosaurus gigas*, the biggest species.

Marine reptiles

Nothosaurus was a marine reptile, not a dinosaur. Yet, like all reptiles, its ancestors evolved on land, developing waterproof skins and other features that enabled them to live in dry habitats. But some reptiles then returned to the water and started developing fish-like adaptations for swimming, just like seals, dolphins, and other modern marine mammals. And like them, they still had to breathe air.

Mid-Triassic seas teemed with life, including both bony fish and sharks. There were also squid and similar animals that would have provided *Nothosaurus* with prey.

FOSSIL FINDS: Europe, North Africa, Asia, Russia, China

FAST FACTS

NAME MEANS:
"southern lizard"
DATE: 245–228 mya

TRIASSIC	JURASSIC	CRETACEOUS
251 MYA	199	145	65 MYA

DIET: Fish-eater

LENGTH: 1.2–3.5 m (4–11 ft)

The feet were webbed, but otherwise the limbs were like those of land animals, with five long toes and stout claws. This indicates that *Nothosaurus* used them for walking as well as swimming. Other nothosaurs had more paddle-like limbs, like those of seals, suggesting that they were more highly adapted to marine life.

It is more than likely that the scaly skin was smooth, more like a dolphin than a crocodile. Camouflage patterns on its back may have helped conceal it from predators in the dappled underwater light, and its belly was probably paler to match the glow from the surface.

Shore breeder

It is likely that *Nothosaurus* bred on the shore, laying eggs like a sea turtle or possibly giving birth to live young like a seal. More advanced marine reptiles such as plesiosaurs and ichthyosaurs gave birth at sea, but they were entirely aquatic, never coming on shore as *Nothosaurus* seems to have done. It may have spent a lot of time on land, like a modern seal, basking on rocks and beaches but hunting in the sea.

Most of *Eoraptor*'s teeth were like serrated blades, ideal for slicing through meat. The theropods that evolved later had these too, but so did many other meat-eating reptiles, so they do not indicate that *Eoraptor* was a theropod. However, it was certainly a hunter.

Eoraptor

This agile, fox-sized animal was one of the first dinosaurs. Its sharp teeth and claws indicate that it was a hunter, and it probably chased lizards and other small animals through the Late Triassic undergrowth of what is now South America. Like most early dinosaurs, *Eoraptor* ran on its hind legs – four-footed forms evolved later – so apart from its size it looks a lot like one of the big meat-eating theropods that were the top predators of the Mesozoic era.

Although long and bristling with teeth, the lower jaw was not very deep and strong. The animal would not have had a very powerful bite, and it probably preyed mainly on small reptiles and the early shrew-like mammals that were just beginning to evolve in the Late Triassic.

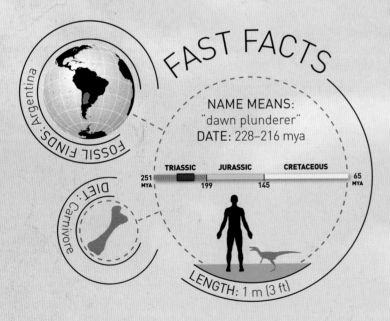

FAST FACTS

FOSSIL FINDS: Argentina

DIET: Carnivore

NAME MEANS: "dawn plunderer"
DATE: 228–216 mya

TRIASSIC	JURASSIC	CRETACEOUS
251 MYA	199	145	65 MYA

LENGTH: 1 m (3 ft)

The eyes faced mainly to the side, so the animal's stereo vision was quite limited. *Eoraptor* did have a good all-round view, however – vital for a small animal at risk from more powerful predators like the much bigger *Herrerasaurus* that lived in the same region.

Valley of the Moon
The remains of *Eoraptor* have been found in northwestern Argentina, in a region known as the Valley of the Moon. It is named for its barren, almost lunar landscape of sandstones and mudstones, laid down by rivers in the Late Triassic. These are the sediments that contain the *Eoraptor* fossils.

The neck of *Eoraptor* was shorter than the necks of similar but later hunters, but it was still long and flexible. This enabled it to snatch fast-moving prey from the ground and possibly from low-growing plants.

Primitive dinosaur
When *Eoraptor* was found, it was identified as an early type of theropod – the group that includes nearly all the later carnivorous dinosaurs. But recent research shows that it was a more primitive type of dinosaur, stemming from a period before the split between the meat-eating theropods and plant-eating sauropodomorphs. This means that it is one of the earliest of the saurischians and one of the most ancestral of all dinosaurs.

No fossil remains of the skin have been found, so we do not know whether *Eoraptor* had scales or simple feathers. However, we do know that it lived in a region with a warm climate. So, if it was warm-blooded, it would not have needed much insulation.

The hind legs were twice as long as the front ones and much more strongly built with powerful muscles. This shows that the animal stood upright, balanced by its long tail. This gave it the agility it needed to chase its prey – and escape its enemies.

Eoraptor ran on its toes, rather like a bird. It stood on three of these toes, but it also had another shorter toe that did not reach the ground. This digitigrade (tiptoe) stance is typical of agile, fast-running animals.

Each hand had five fingers, although two were much shorter than the others. Each of the three long fingers had a sharp, sturdy claw that the animal may have used to seize prey and hold it while it got to work with its teeth. But the claws had other uses as well, such as searching vegetation and defending against enemies.

Coelophysis

This slim, lightweight hunter is the best known of a group of small meat-eating dinosaurs that flourished during the Late Triassic and Early Jurassic periods. They were among the earliest theropods – the dinosaurs that were the main predators throughout the Mesozoic era – although their own particular line died out in the Jurassic. *Coelophysis* itself competed for prey with many much bigger, more powerful hunters that were not dinosaurs at all, but giant relatives of crocodilians that dominated life on land during the Triassic.

FAST FACTS

FOSSIL FINDS: North America, Southern Africa, China

DIET: Carnivore

NAME MEANS:
"hollow form"
DATE: 228–183 mya

TRIASSIC	JURASSIC	CRETACEOUS
251 MYA	199	145

LENGTH: 3 m (10 ft)

The skull of *Coelophysis* was long and narrow, with equally long jaws and a shallow jawbone. The jaws were well suited to snapping up small prey, but may not have been strong enough for seizing large, powerful animals.

Its long, flexible, mobile neck allowed *Coelophysis* to rapidly dart its head forward to snatch small animals before they had a chance to dive for cover. This was to become a typical feature of all the smaller, more agile theropod hunters of the Mesozoic era.

Although it stood on strong hind legs like all theropods, *Coelophysis* had long front limbs. It had three functional fingers with stout claws for seizing prey. It also had a very short and probably almost useless fourth finger.

Like most hunters, *Coelophysis* had sharp vision for locating and catching prey. Bones found inside its remains indicate that it hunted small, fast-moving reptiles.

Mass burial

This dinosaur is unusually well known because so many of its skeletons have been found. In 1947, more than 500 *Coelophysis* skeletons were discovered at Ghost Ranch in New Mexico. Most of the animals seem to have died together, possibly because they were drowned by a flash flood. It is likely that they gathered at the site to drink during a drought and were suddenly overwhelmed and buried by a torrent of water and mud.

A long tail helped with balance when running, and its slim build and strong hind legs suggest that *Coelophysis* was quick on its feet. Like all theropods, it had hollow limb bones, saving weight and making it more agile.

Coelophysis had more than 100 small, sharp-pointed teeth in its upper and lower jaws. They were curved, saw-edged blades, ideal for dealing with small prey. It may also have scavenged meat from the carcasses of bigger animals.

Plateosaurus

While one branch of the saurischian dinosaurs evolved into meat-eating theropods like *Coelophysis*, another gave rise to plant-eating sauropodomorphs such as *Plateosaurus*. This was one of the prosauropods, which were the main herbivores of the Late Triassic. Although bigger than most of them, *Plateosaurus* was a lot lighter than the colossal sauropods of the Jurassic, and unlike them, it probably walked on its hind legs. *Plateosaurus* seems to have been common in what is now Europe. Many skeletons have been found together, indicating that it lived in herds, migrating over the plains in search of food.

FAST FACTS

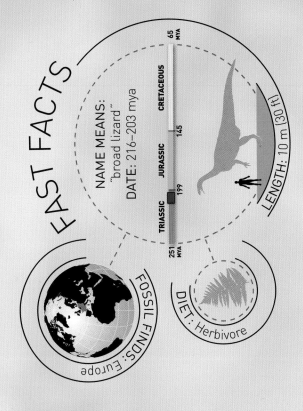

NAME MEANS: "broad lizard"
DATE: 216–203 mya

TRIASSIC | JURASSIC | CRETACEOUS
251 MYA | 199 | 145 | 65 MYA

LENGTH: 10 m (30 ft)

FOSSIL FINDS: Europe

DIET: Herbivore

Like other prosauropods, this animal ate mostly plants, reaching up to browse on cycads and conifers. Its small, slicing teeth overlapped like scissor blades to shear through leaf stems and had rough surfaces for shredding the tough foliage.

With its long neck, *Plateosaurus* could get at leaves that were out of reach of other Triassic plant-eaters. Its main competitors were other prosauropods, but most of these were smaller. Its high vantage point also gave it early warning of any approaching threats.

Hands and feet

The prosauropods evolved from much smaller meat-eating dinosaurs, and the smallest ones probably resembled *Eoraptor* – an early two-footed hunter. During the Late Triassic and Early Jurassic, they evolved larger and larger forms, which may have spent more time on all fours. Despite this, they all had distinct hands with long fingers and thumbs rather than weight-supporting front feet like the later sauropods.

The skin seems to have been tough and scaly, like that of a large lizard. The scales protected the skin from scratches and helped prevent moisture loss. This was important in the Triassic, when the climate was hot and dry. It may have enabled *Plateosaurus* herds to make long treks through arid terrain.

Favoured sites

Plateosaurus is the best known of the prosauropods, and one of the most common dinosaur fossils. Dozens of skeletons preserved in Triassic sandstones have been unearthed in more than 50 locations in Europe. Some of these sites may have been favoured feeding or breeding areas, with herds of animals returning year after year. Alternatively, the bones could have been washed together by floodwater.

Although shorter than its hind limbs, its front limbs were long enough to allow *Plateosaurus* to lean on its hands to feed on low-growing plants. But recent research shows that it could not turn the palms of its hands downwards, so it could not easily walk on them.

A long, heavy tail balanced the front end of the body, enabling the animal to walk on its hind legs and rear up to feed.

The hands could grasp branches when feeding.

Long, powerful legs supported the animal's weight and allowed it to reach high into the treetops. It could probably run on its hind legs, and despite its size and weight, *Plateosaurus* may have been able to move quite fast.

The powerful thumb claw might have been used for defence or fights between rival males.

These animals mostly propelled themselves with their tails, but would have used the long flippers for turning and small manoeuvres.

Bone bed
Shonisaurus is known mainly from a single site in Nevada, USA. A mass of bones found in the 1920s turned out to be the skeletons of 37 of these giant animals, the biggest being 15 m (50 ft) long. Much later, in the 1990s, the bones of a similar animal were discovered in British Columbia, Canada – but it was even bigger at 21 m (70 ft). This makes it the largest marine reptile ever found, although smaller than a blue whale.

Shonisaurus

The ichthyosaurs were a group of dolphin-like marine reptiles that flourished in the world's oceans throughout much of the Mesozoic era, but disappeared some 90 million years ago. This was one of the biggest – a whale-sized beast that lived in the Late Triassic. It probably hunted fish, as well as squid and similar creatures such as ammonites. Like all ichthyosaurs, *Shonisaurus* would have spent its entire life at sea, although like any reptile, it had to breathe air.

Big *Shonisaurus* skulls do not have any teeth, and smaller ones have them only at the front of their jaws. It seems that the animal did not need teeth and lost them with age.

Lazy giant
Although one of the biggest ichthyosaurs, *Shonisaurus* was relatively primitive. Later ones, such as *Ichthyosaurus* itself, were more dolphin-like, with bigger tail fins. They could swim much faster to catch prey and escape danger.

The tail was formed from a fleshy fin above a downturned extension of the backbone. It was rather like the tail of a typical shark, but the other way up – and since the fin was quite small, it would almost certainly have been far less useful for propulsion.

The long, narrow snout was shaped like the bill of a large bird. It could be swung easily from side to side to snatch passing prey, because it did not offer much resistance to the water.

As with other ichthyosaurs, the eyes were set in large sockets, each enclosed by a bony ring. This may have protected the eye from damage when hunting or helped resist intense water pressure during deep diving.

The flippers were much longer and narrower than those of most ichthyosaurs. Each had a complex skeleton made up of many small bones.

FAST FACTS

FOSSIL FINDS: North America

DIET: Fish-eater

NAME MEANS: "lizard of the Shoshone Mountains"
DATE: 216–203 mya

TRIASSIC	JURASSIC	CRETACEOUS
251 MYA	199	145	65 MYA

LENGTH: 21 m (70 ft)

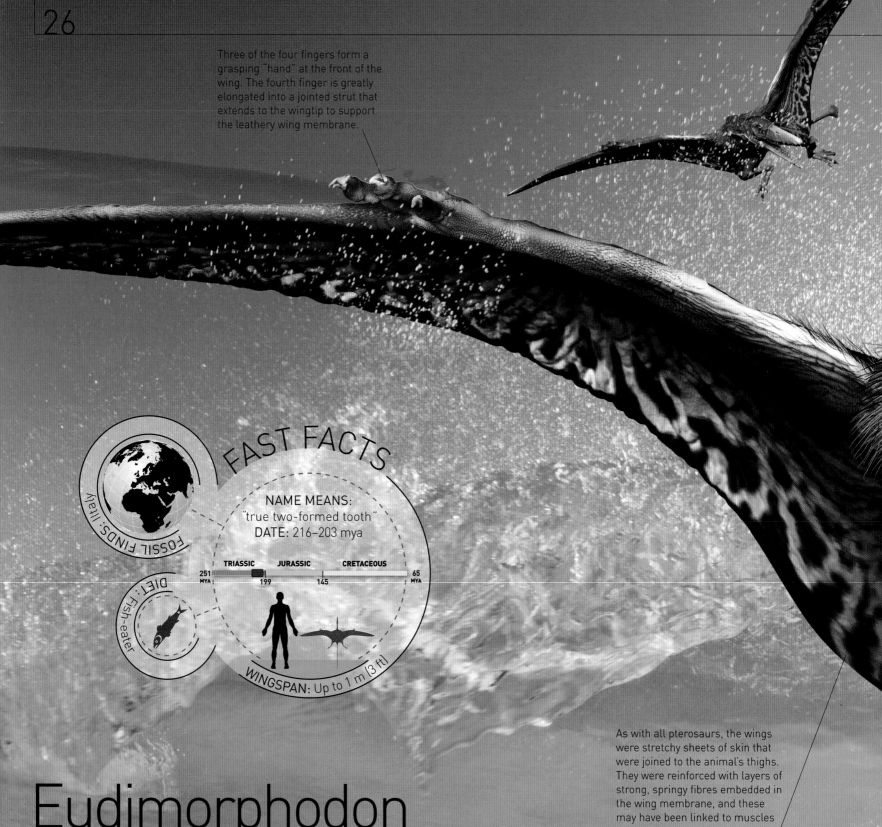

Three of the four fingers form a grasping "hand" at the front of the wing. The fourth finger is greatly elongated into a jointed strut that extends to the wingtip to support the leathery wing membrane.

FAST FACTS

FOSSIL FINDS: Italy

DIET: Fish-eater

NAME MEANS:
"true two-formed tooth"
DATE: 216–203 mya

TRIASSIC	JURASSIC	CRETACEOUS
251 MYA		65 MYA
199	145	

WINGSPAN: Up to 1 m (3 ft)

As with all pterosaurs, the wings were stretchy sheets of skin that were joined to the animal's thighs. They were reinforced with layers of strong, springy fibres embedded in the wing membrane, and these may have been linked to muscles that could adjust the wing profile.

Eudimorphodon

Long before the birds evolved, there were other vertebrate animals hunting in the Mesozoic skies. They were pterosaurs – close relatives of the dinosaurs – which appeared in the Late Triassic. *Eudimorphodon* was one of the earliest, a crow-sized flying reptile with a long tail and a large head bristling with sharp teeth. These were of two main types, which explains its odd name. They indicate that it was a fish-eater, and fish remains have been found among its fossils. It probably hunted along lake and seashores and over coastal lagoons.

Elusive ancestors

Pterosaurs seem to have appeared almost fully formed in the Triassic. Early ones like *Eudimorphodon* were clearly able to fly well, so they must have had flying ancestors, but the fossil evidence for this is proving very difficult to find. This is probably because these animals had slim, delicate bones that did not survive long enough to become fossils.

Pterosaur teeth

Compared to most dinosaurs, the Triassic pterosaurs had unusually complex teeth, with each animal having teeth of different shapes for specific jobs. Some later pterosaurs had teeth specialized for filtering food from the water or crushing shellfish, while others had no teeth at all.

The body of *Eudimorphodon* was covered by a dense coat of fur-like fibres. These would have helped insulate it and stop it from losing body heat. They show that *Eudimorphodon* was warm-blooded, as you would expect for a large flying animal that needed a lot of stamina to stay airborne.

Like other Triassic pterosaurs, *Eudimorphodon* had a long tail. This probably had a small diamond-shaped vane on the end that would have helped it make tight turns in the air. Later pterosaurs had much shorter tails, with no vane.

Strong hind legs with stout claws would have enabled the animal to forage for food on the ground. It probably walked on both its back and front limbs, folding its wings up out of the way.

Eudimorphodon had long, fang-like teeth at the front of its mouth, ideal for seizing slippery fish. It had smaller, multi-pointed teeth at the back of its mouth, which it would have used to cut its prey into smaller chunks that were easy to swallow.

Compared to later sauropods, *Isanosaurus* had a short neck. But it could probably rear up on its hind legs to feed, and this helped it reach high into the treetops.

Like all animals that eat a lot of leaves, *Isanosaurus* needed a bulky digestive system. Big bones in its pelvis – found in all sauropods – meant that this was carried well forward of the animal's hind legs, so it had good reason to support some of its weight on its front feet when walking.

Long vertical extensions of the vertebrae – the bones of the spine – were linked by muscles and tendons that supported the back and tail.

Sauropod herds
These big herbivores almost certainly lived in herds, much as wild bison and elephants do today. We know about this from the evidence of trackways – long lines of fossil footprints left in mud that eventually turned to rock. The animals would have roamed the landscape to find places where there was plenty of food. Many later herbivores seem to have made seasonal migrations between different feeding and breeding areas.

The front legs were long, but not as long or massive as the hind legs. The front feet also had more mobile toes that may have been useful when feeding high in the trees.

Each hind foot was supported by a big wedge-shaped pad of fatty tissue, rather like the foot of an elephant. This spread the load, leaving a broad oval footprint.

Isanosaurus

The Late Triassic saw the evolution of new types of plant-eating sauropodomorphs. Instead of walking on their hind legs like prosauropods, these creatures walked on all fours. This helped support their bodies, and enabled some of their descendants to grow into the biggest, heaviest land animals of all time. They were the sauropods. One of the earliest was *Isanosaurus*, which lived in what is now southeast Asia. It was a lot smaller than later giants, but it probably had the same way of life.

Although its skull has not been found, *Isanosaurus* probably had a small head with short jaws and leaf-shaped or spoon-like teeth for cropping leaves.

Despite its weight, *Isanosaurus* walked on its toes.

Skeletal evidence
The fossils of *Isanosaurus* are among the earliest known for any sauropod. Only a few bones have survived, but the tall-spined vertebrae are not like those of earlier prosauropods, and its thigh bones are straighter and more like those of later giants. So scientists are confident that it is one of the first true sauropods.

FAST FACTS

FOSSIL FINDS: Thailand

DIET: Herbivore

NAME MEANS:
"northern Thailand lizard"
DATE: 216–199 mya

	TRIASSIC	JURASSIC	CRETACEOUS	
251 MYA		199	145	65 MYA

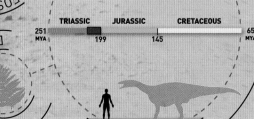

LENGTH: 6 m (20 ft)

Jurassic world

The Jurassic was the second period of the Mesozoic era, which lasted from 199 to 145 million years ago. During this period, the vast supercontinent of Pangaea split in two, changing the climate and allowing lush vegetation and animal life to colonize much more of the land. This enabled the dinosaurs and pterosaurs to flourish over a larger area. The dinosaurs evolved into a spectacular variety of forms, becoming the dominant large land animals. This was the period that saw the evolution of the huge plant-eating sauropods and the first really big meat-eating theropods. A branch of the theropod line also gave rise to the birds, which are still with us. Meanwhile, the marine reptiles evolved as fearsome predators that dominated life in the oceans.

Continents and seas

As the Tethys Ocean grew wider, it split Pangaea into two main blocks – Laurasia and Gondwana. Meanwhile, the Panthalassic Ocean shrank to form the Pacific. Rising sea levels flooded continental margins with shallow seas, dividing large landmasses into smaller ones. As animals were isolated from each other by the water, they evolved in different ways.

A rift extending west from the Tethys Ocean divided north and south.

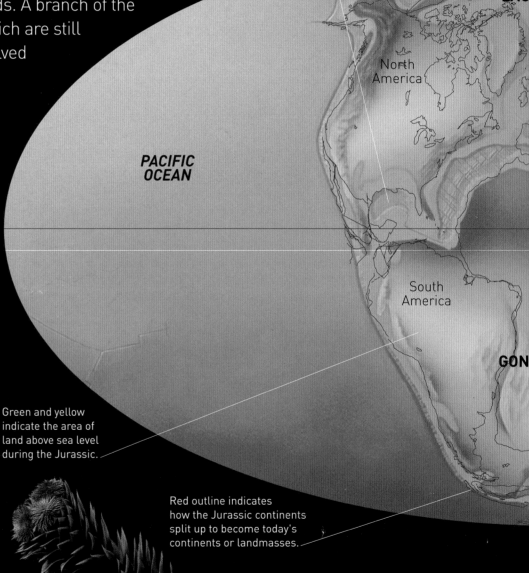

PACIFIC OCEAN

Alaska

LAU

North America

South America

GON

Green and yellow indicate the area of land above sea level during the Jurassic.

Red outline indicates how the Jurassic continents split up to become today's continents or landmasses.

Climate

The arid heart of the giant Pangaean landmass was eliminated as the supercontinent was split by the expanding Tethys Ocean. This made the climate much wetter and milder than in the Triassic and allowed forests to grow in regions that had once been dry and barren.

Plant life

During the Jurassic, plant life was more lush and widespread than in the Triassic, But the plants were similar, consisting of horsetails, ferns, clubmosses, ginkgos, cycads, and conifer trees like this monkey puzzle. There were still no flowering plants of any kind, and certainly no grasses.

Dinosaurs

At the end of the Triassic, a lot of the dinosaurs' competitors became extinct. This gave dinosaurs the chance to take over by evolving new forms that were suited to different ways of life. This process eventually gave rise to giant plant-eating sauropods, more powerful theropod hunters, plated stegosaurs like this *Huayangosaurus*, heavily armoured ankylosaurs, and the earliest ornithopods.

Siberia

SIA

Europe

North China

South China

Turkey   Iran   Tibet

Indochina

The northern continent of Laurasia was split by many shallow seas.

frica

Arabia

TETHYS OCEAN

ANA

India

Australia

Antarctica

The southern continent of Gondwana formed the largest landmass.

Land invertebrates

Insects of many kinds flourished in the Jurassic forests, but since there were no flowering plants, there were no nectar-feeding insects such as butterflies and bees. There were definitely dragonflies, cockroaches, beetles, and flies, which were either hunters or fed on plants and dead material. There were also many other invertebrates such as spiders and scorpions that preyed on the insects, and myriapods resembling this modern pill millipede.

Protosuchus

Life in the water

The shallow seas that formed on the continental margins teemed with life, particularly ammonites and belemnites, which were relatives of modern squid. These were hunted by a variety of fish, and both were eaten by marine reptiles such as this *Ichthyosaurus*. In turn, the smaller ichthyosaurs were preyed upon by giant plesiosaurs.

Triassic survivors

The extinction event at the end of the Triassic eliminated nearly all the big land animals except the dinosaurs and crocodylomorphs such as *Protosuchus*. The other main group of large Jurassic land animals were the pterosaurs. Early mammals were around, but were quite small.

Big eyes on the sides of its head gave *Lesothosaurus* an excellent all-round view of any approaching threats. Such wariness is typical of small plant-eaters.

Behind a beak were simple pointed teeth. These seem adapted for slicing through leaves and stems rather than grinding them to a pulp. This made the leaves less easy to digest, so *Lesothosaurus* may have eaten insects or carrion as well.

Powerful hind legs would have given *Lesothosaurus* a good turn of speed to escape its enemies, like a modern gazelle. It had four toes, but only three touched the ground.

The animal's front limbs were a lot shorter than its back ones, so they were not used for walking. Instead, they had long, grasping fingers.

Lesothosaurus

The first ornithischian dinosaurs were small animals that walked on two legs, so although they were plant-eaters, they looked a little like the carnivorous theropods. *Lesothosaurus* is one of the earliest known, with simple teeth that were poorly adapted for pulping leaves, unlike those of many later ornithischians. Yet it was probably fast and agile, giving it a good chance of escaping hunters like this *Sphenosuchus*.

Primitive feature

The teeth of most ornithischian dinosaurs were inset from the sides of their jaws. This indicates that they had cheeks like ours, which stopped food from falling out of the sides of their mouths when chewing. *Lesothosaurus* does not have this feature, showing that it was a very primitive type of ornithischian.

Beak bone

All ornithischian dinosaurs had a special toothless bone at the tip of the lower jaw that helped support a beak. *Lesothosaurus* was one of the earliest dinosaurs with this adaptation, which may have made it more efficient at gathering plant food.

FAST FACTS

NAME MEANS:
"lizard from Lesotho"
DATE: 199–189 mya

TRIASSIC	JURASSIC	CRETACEOUS

251 MYA — 199 — 145 — 65 MYA

FOSSIL FINDS: South Africa

DIET: Herbivore

LENGTH: 1 m (3 ft)

Like any animal that eats a lot of leaves, *Lesothosaurus* needed a big, heavy digestive system. But this was carried well back in its body, owing to the shape of its ornithischian pelvis. This meant that its weight was balanced over its hips, allowing it to walk and run on its hind legs.

Heterodontosaurus

This small Early Jurassic dinosaur looks like a typical plant-eating ornithischian, except for one thing – its teeth. Most dinosaurs had teeth that were all very similar, but *Heterodontosaurus* had closely packed chewing teeth at the back of its mouth and long, pointed teeth at the front. The pointed teeth are like the canines of modern carnivores such as dogs, suggesting that it may have used them for eating meat. Yet other ornithischians ate plants, so this seems unlikely. Their true function is still a mystery.

The jaws were tipped with a horny beak, like those of other ornithischians. The beak was almost certainly used for gathering leaves.

Key discovery
The first fossil of *Heterodontosaurus* was discovered in South Africa in 1962. It was a single skull and jaw, but with most of its extraordinary teeth in place. A complete skeleton unearthed 14 years later is one of the finest ever found, with every bone intact.

The long, tapering tail acted as a counterbalance.

Heterodontosaurus had sturdy front limbs with strong, grasping hands, each with five clawed fingers. It may have used these to seize small animals as part of its diet.

A Jurassic pig?
Although the long, pointed teeth of *Heterodontosaurus* make it look like a fierce hunter, it probably fed mainly on plants. It was well equipped for chewing, which the predatory theropods were not, and it may have used its long teeth to dig up juicy roots or for defence. But it could have eaten small animals, too. Many modern mammals such as wild pigs have mixed diets, and maybe this was their Jurassic equivalent.

FOSSIL FINDS: South Africa

DIET: Mainly a herbivore

FAST FACTS

NAME MEANS:
"different-toothed lizard"
DATE: 199–189 mya

TRIASSIC	JURASSIC	CRETACEOUS	
251 MYA	199	145	65 MYA

LENGTH: 1 m (3 ft)

We do not know what the skin of this dinosaur was like, but it was probably scaly. Camouflage colours and patterns would have helped it hide from predators.

Roughly the size of a turkey, this animal stood on two legs. Being light and agile, it could probably run quite fast to get away from its enemies.

Big eyes on the sides of its head would have given *Heterodontosaurus* excellent all-round vision to check for danger while feeding.

A deep notch in the upper jaw made space for the very long lower "canine" teeth. These were almost like tusks, and it is possible that they were used for fighting.

Cryolophosaurus

This big meat-eater is distinctive because it had a peculiar bony crest on top of its tall, narrow skull. Instead of running along its forehead, as with a few other crested theropods, it ran across the animal's head, just above its eyes. The crest was probably brightly coloured and almost certainly played a part in dominance displays between rivals like these. A stronger animal may have had a more impressive crest. Apart from this odd feature, *Cryolophosaurus* is also unusual because its fossils were found in Antarctica, in one of the few ice-free regions of the Transantarctic Mountains.

The teeth were curved serrated blades, like those of most hunters. It also had a deep, strong jaw.

Crested theropods
During the Early Jurassic, dinosaurs began to diversify into many new forms of plant-eaters and hunters. *Cryolophosaurus* belonged to a theropod group called the dilophosaurids, which were all distinguished by crests on their heads. They flourished in the Early Jurassic, but then died out. Their place was taken by more advanced stiff-tailed theropods known as the tetanurans.

Unlike the tetanuran theropods that became so successful during the Late Jurassic and Cretaceous, *Cryolophosaurus* had four fingers on each hand instead of three. It may have used its hands to help seize prey.

The bones of a large plant-eating dinosaur known as *Glacialisaurus* were found near the remains of *Cryolophosaurus*. This animal may have been its main prey. Other bones included those of pterosaurs and small mammals.

The crest was curled over like a quiff of hair, and before it was given an official name, the dinosaur was known as "Elvisaurus", after Elvis Presley!

Despite its large head and jaws, *Cryolophosaurus* had a relatively slender, lightweight build. It was probably a fast runner.

FAST FACTS

FOSSIL FINDS: Antarctica

DIET: Carnivore

NAME MEANS:
"frozen crested lizard"
DATE: 189–183 mya

TRIASSIC	JURASSIC	CRETACEOUS
251 MYA	199	145	65 MYA

LENGTH: 6 m (20 ft)

Buried treasure
Antarctic dinosaur fossils may be quite common, because in Early Jurassic times the continent lay much further north and had a temperate climate with cycad and conifer forests. However, most of the rocks that might bear fossils are now buried beneath thick ice sheets.

Scelidosaurus

The Early Jurassic saw the emergence of the first armoured dinosaurs – the thyreophorans. Later, these evolved into the plated stegosaurs and tank-like ankylosaurs, but early ones like *Scelidosaurus* just had small bony plates embedded in their skin. These plates, or scutes, were covered with tough keratin – the material that fingernails are made of. They were not connected to each other, so they did not form a rigid shield, but they would have posed a problem for any enemy. However, they would also have weighed the animal down, giving it less chance of running away.

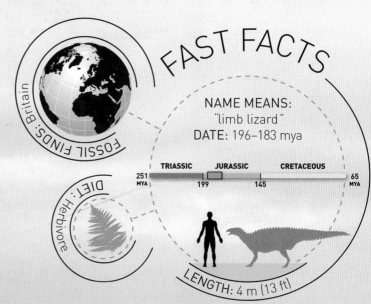

FAST FACTS

FOSSIL FINDS: Britain

DIET: Herbivore

NAME MEANS:
"limb lizard"
DATE: 196–183 mya

	TRIASSIC	JURASSIC	CRETACEOUS	
251 MYA		199	145	65 MYA

LENGTH: 4 m (13 ft)

Defensive weapons
The main enemies of the plant-eating dinosaurs during the Early Jurassic were slender, fast theropods with blade-like teeth. If one of these attacked a *Scelidosaurus*, it would have broken its teeth on the bony scutes. But *Scelidosaurus* did not just rely on its armour for defence. It had a long tail that was also studded with bony plates. A single well-aimed blow with this would have crippled any attacker.

The bony scutes were tall knobs, almost like spikes. They formed several rows that extended down the animal's back – from its head to the tip of its tail. In between, the skin was covered with small, flat, non-overlapping scales.

It is more than likely that *Scelidosaurus* lived in herds that travelled together in search of good feeding grounds. Living like this would have been safer, especially for younger animals that would have been easier targets for hungry hunters.

The long front limbs indicate that *Scelidosaurus* walked on all fours, unlike earlier ornithischians. Its heavy armour would certainly have encouraged this. All the later thyreophorans have the same four-footed gait.

Acid solution

Scelidosaurus was one of the first dinosaur skeletons to be found in the world. It was unearthed in Britain in 1858. The fossil was buried in very hard limestone that was so difficult to remove that most of it stayed hidden for more than a century. But limestone can be dissolved by acid, and years of work using this technique have now revealed the entire skeleton.

The short, horny beak at the tip of the snout was backed up by small leaf-shaped or pointed teeth. The animal would have gathered food by browsing on low-growing plants.

The immense length of *Barosaurus* enabled it to reach up to at least 15 m (49 ft) and browse in treetops that were beyond the reach of other ground-based herbivores.

Barosaurus

This dinosaur was one of the colossal plant-eating sauropods of the Jurassic. From head to tail, sauropods were the longest land animals that ever existed – especially *Barosaurus*, which had a particularly long neck. This enabled it to gather leaves from high in the tree canopy. What's more, its powerful hips, short body, and short forelimbs suggest that it often reared up on its hind legs to reach even higher.

FOSSIL FINDS: North America

DIET: Herbivore

NAME MEANS:
"heavy lizard"
DATE: 155–145 mya

TRIASSIC	JURASSIC	CRETACEOUS
251 MYA	199	145	65 MYA

LENGTH: 27 m (88 ft)

The very long whiplash tail might have made an effective defensive weapon against predators such as *Allosaurus*, which lived in the same habitat.

Food processor
These animals could not chew their food to make it easier to digest. Scientists used to think that they swallowed stones to help grind up the food in their gizzards (muscular stomachs), but there is no clear evidence of this. It is more likely that they gulped down vast amounts of leafy food and relied on bacteria living in their digestive systems to process it by fermentation. Some modern leaf-eating animals, such as the koala, use a similar system.

A row of spines extending all the way down the animal's back may have been a decorative crest or a defence feature. These spines were not part of the skeleton, but were bony plates embedded in the skin.

Like all the diplodocids – named after *Diplodocus*, the most well known – *Barosaurus* had a very small head for its size. Its skull was relatively long and narrow, with a small cranium but a broad snout.

The eyes were set well back in its head, giving a good all-round view, especially when feeding high in the trees.

The skin was scaly. This provided protection from scratches and helped reduce moisture loss. If the animal was warm-blooded, it would not have needed much insulation because its bulk would retain body heat.

All the teeth were at the front of the jaw. The animal may have used them like a rake to rip leaves off twigs.

The massive pillar-like hind legs were like those of elephants, with the heels supported by wedges of fatty, fibrous tissue. Each forefoot had a single large claw.

Plates and spines

During the Jurassic period, some plant-eating dinosaurs developed a form of armour as protection against big killer theropods. Over time the armour became more elaborate, and while it remained partly defensive, it also became important for display and ritual combat between rivals, like the antlers of modern deer. The result was a wonderful variety of flamboyant plates, spines, and frills.

Dorsal plates

Most of the armoured dinosaurs belonged to a group of ornithischians called the thyreophorans. They included the stegosaurs – spectacular animals with rows of plates and spines along their backs. *Kentrosaurus* was one of several that also had long spikes on its shoulders.

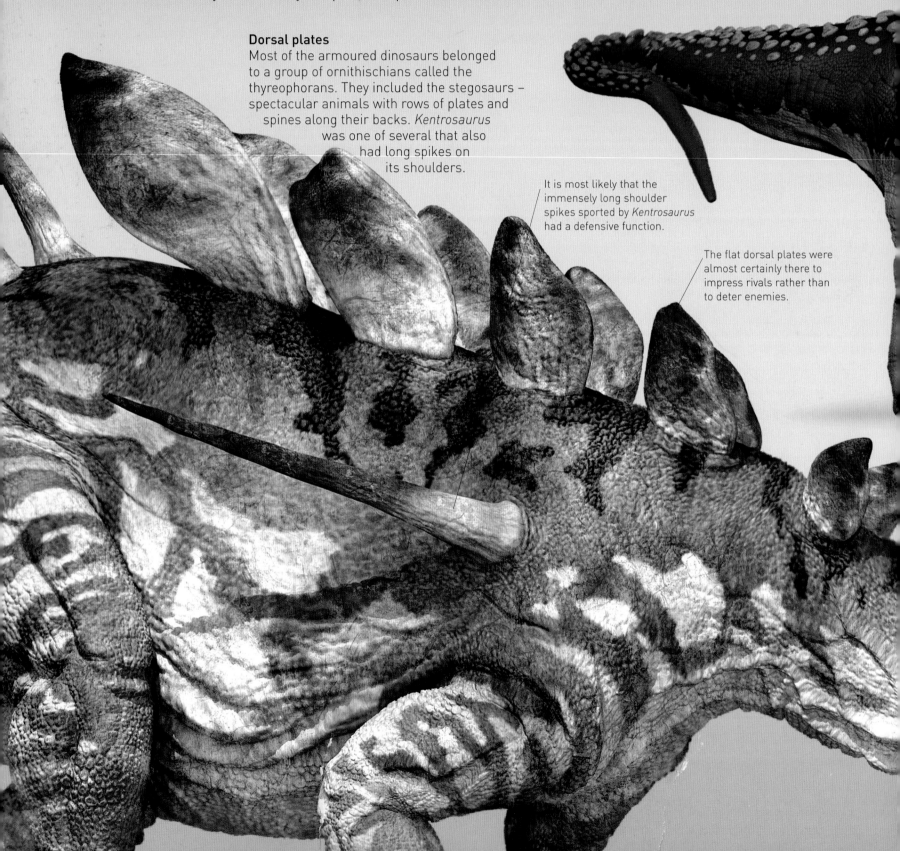

Many of the scutes studding *Gastonia*'s back and tail were extended into blade-like plates.

It is most likely that the immensely long shoulder spikes sported by *Kentrosaurus* had a defensive function.

The flat dorsal plates were almost certainly there to impress rivals rather than to deter enemies.

Heavy armour

Closely allied to the plated stegosaurs and part of the same thyreophoran group, ankylosaurs such as *Gastonia* were low-slung heavyweights with thick bony scutes on their backs. Their armour was clearly for protection, and some ankylosaurs had massive bony clubs on the tips of their tails.

Six big spikes and many smaller knobs adorned the neck frill, which may have been vividly coloured.

The flat bony plates dotting the skin of *Saltasaurus* were for defence, not show.

While impressive, the long nose horn may have been a defensive feature.

Frills and horns

In the Cretaceous, one ornithischian group developed bony neck frills that may have anchored extra-powerful jaw muscles. They evolved into extravagantly frilled and horned ceratopsians such as *Styracosaurus*, with its extraordinary array of spiky ornaments.

Defensive studs

Most armoured dinosaurs were ornithischians, but many of the Cretaceous sauropods known as titanosaurs had bony studs embedded in their skin. These would have given them some defence against the huge predators of the time.

Devil's crown

Several of the Late Cretaceous pachycephalosaurs, or "boneheads", had various knobs and spikes crowning their thickened skulls. One of the most spectacular was *Stygimoloch*. Its name means "horned devil from the river of death" – a reference to the Hell Creek fossil site in Montana, USA, where its was found. Its spiky crown may have been useful in defence, but it was probably used for threat displays against rivals.

Stegosaurus

This well-known dinosaur was the biggest of the stegosaurs, one of the two main groups of armoured thyreophorans. The stegosaurs were among the most common dinosaurs of the Late Jurassic, and their bones have been found all over the world. Their most distinctive features were the bony plates that sprouted from their backs. *Stegosaurus* itself had huge flat plates, but others had smaller plates or even spikes, and many had long spikes on their shoulders. Similar spikes on their tails would have been used for defence, but scientists still puzzle over the function of the plates.

FAST FACTS

NAME MEANS: "roof lizard"
DATE: 155–145 mya

TRIASSIC   JURASSIC   CRETACEOUS
251 MYA   199   145   65 MYA

LENGTH: 9 m (30 ft)

FOSSIL FINDS: North America and Portugal

DIET: Herbivore

Puzzling plates

When *Stegosaurus* was first found in the 1870s by the fossil hunter Othniel Marsh, he thought its plates lay flat on its back, like roof tiles. This explains its odd name. A century later, some scientists suggested that the plates absorbed or lost heat, depending on how the animal stood, helping it regulate its temperature. Most scientists now think they were display features, like flamboyant bird plumage.

The front limbs were a lot shorter than the back ones, so *Stegosaurus* walked with its hips much higher than its shoulders. The bones of its spine were also very tall, and this gave the animal a high, arched shape. The huge alternating plates on its back added to this effect and made it look much bigger than it actually was.

The plates were not part of the skeleton, but were attached to the skin by pads of tough cartilage. They were probably sheathed with horny keratin. The plates of some stegosaurs were paired, but *Stegosaurus* plates formed an alternating double row.

Four big spikes stuck out sideways from the tip of the tail. *Stegosaurus* would have used these to defend itself by making crippling sideswipes at any attacking theropod, such as *Allosaurus*.

Stegosaurus had a long head with a narrow snout, tipped with a toothless horny beak. It probably used this to crop low-growing plants, which it then sliced up – rather than chewed – with its many small, leaf-shaped teeth.

The neck was protected by flexible armour made of small bony plates embedded in its skin, a little like medieval chain mail. This made it difficult for a predator to kill it by going for its throat.

Allosaurus

Big predatory theropods appeared in the Middle Jurassic with the advent of the carnosaurs – fearsome hunters with knife-edged teeth that were specialized for attacking the stegosaurs and huge plant-eating sauropods of the time. One of the best known is *Allosaurus*, a giant killer that loosely resembled *Tyrannosaurus* but lived 70 million years earlier.

Slashing teeth

Although it was clearly a top predator that hunted big animals, *Allosaurus* did not have very powerful jaw muscles. It is possible that it attacked by opening its jaws very wide and slashing at its prey with its knife-edged teeth. They would have acted like a saw blade, slicing through flesh and causing massive blood loss, and the victim would have soon collapsed.

The long, pointed teeth were flattened from side to side with sharp serrated edges, like curved dagger blades. Teeth like this are ideal for slicing through meat, but are not particularly strong. So *Allosaurus* would have targeted the softer parts of its victims, avoiding their bones.

Like all its close relatives, *Allosaurus* had a pair of bony ridges running down its snout. These may have strengthened the skull. But it also had a short triangular horn in front of each eye, and these horns were almost certainly just for show.

The jaw and skull of *Allosaurus* were very deep and narrow, and it could gape its mouth wide open to take huge bites. Its skull had big openings in the sides that made it lighter, but they reduced its strength. The openings may have contained air sacs that were linked to its lungs, as in modern birds.

FAST FACTS

NAME MEANS: "different lizard"

DATE: 155–145 mya

TRIASSIC	JURASSIC	CRETACEOUS
251 MYA	199 · 145	65 MYA

LENGTH: 12 m (39 ft)

FOSSIL FINDS: North America and Portugal

DIET: Carnivore

Sticky trap

Allosaurus seems to have been one of the most common large predators of the Late Jurassic. Just one site in Utah, USA, yielded the bones of more than 40 of them. It was once an area of sticky mud that trapped prey animals, attracting hungry hunters who became trapped in their turn.

The animal stood on long, powerful hind limbs, like all theropods. These seem to have been built for speed as well as strength.

The strong forelimbs had three-fingered hands armed with powerful claws, each up to 15 cm (6 in) long. *Allosaurus* probably used them like meat hooks to cling to its prey. They would have been especially useful when attacking big sauropods.

Allosaurus had four toes, with a small one pointing back and three much bigger toes pointing forwards. This toe arrangement helped spread its weight.

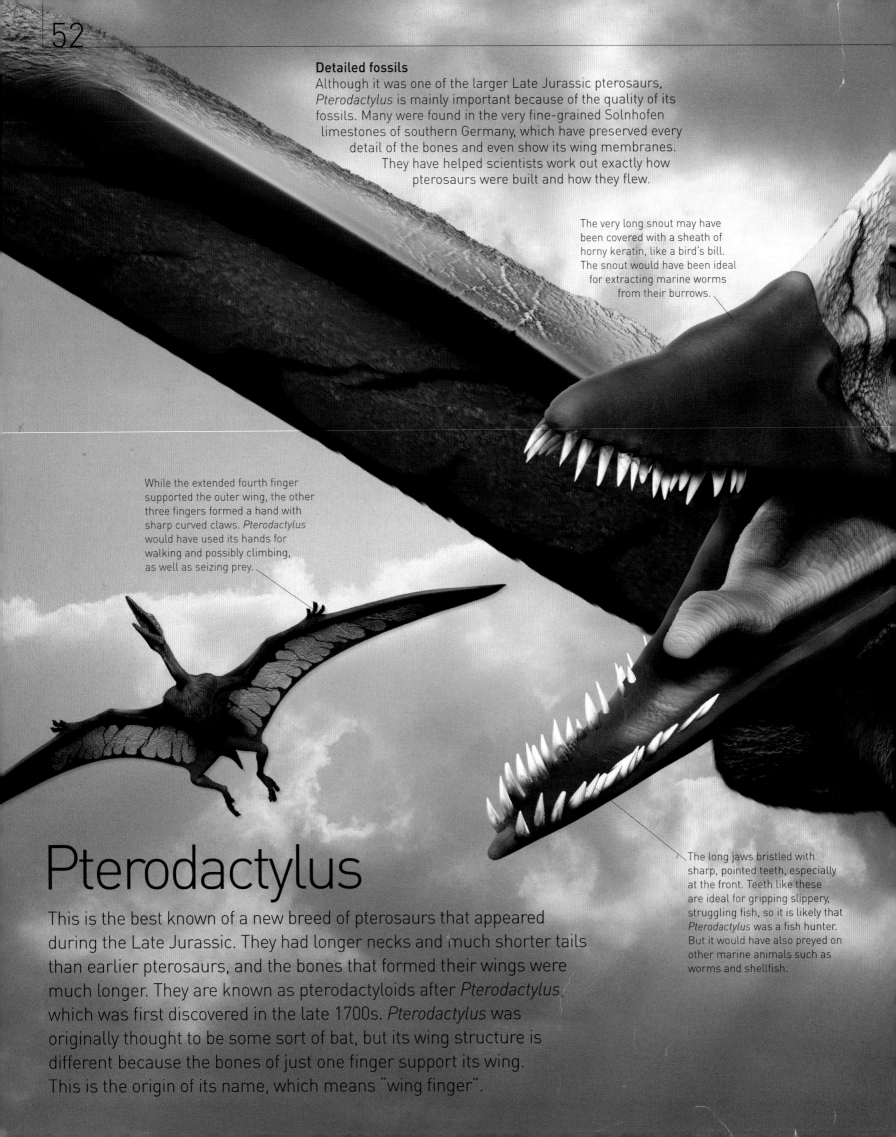

Detailed fossils
Although it was one of the larger Late Jurassic pterosaurs, *Pterodactylus* is mainly important because of the quality of its fossils. Many were found in the very fine-grained Solnhofen limestones of southern Germany, which have preserved every detail of the bones and even show its wing membranes. They have helped scientists work out exactly how pterosaurs were built and how they flew.

The very long snout may have been covered with a sheath of horny keratin, like a bird's bill. The snout would have been ideal for extracting marine worms from their burrows.

While the extended fourth finger supported the outer wing, the other three fingers formed a hand with sharp curved claws. *Pterodactylus* would have used its hands for walking and possibly climbing, as well as seizing prey.

Pterodactylus

This is the best known of a new breed of pterosaurs that appeared during the Late Jurassic. They had longer necks and much shorter tails than earlier pterosaurs, and the bones that formed their wings were much longer. They are known as pterodactyloids after *Pterodactylus*, which was first discovered in the late 1700s. *Pterodactylus* was originally thought to be some sort of bat, but its wing structure is different because the bones of just one finger support its wing. This is the origin of its name, which means "wing finger".

The long jaws bristled with sharp, pointed teeth, especially at the front. Teeth like these are ideal for gripping slippery, struggling fish, so it is likely that *Pterodactylus* was a fish hunter. But it would have also preyed on other marine animals such as worms and shellfish.

One *Pterodactylus* fossil found in 1998 clearly shows a lightweight crest of soft skin-like tissue on the skull. This would have been a display feature, like the crests sported by many modern birds, suggesting that it was also brightly coloured.

The wings were membranes of skin and muscle. They were supported by the bones of the fourth finger and by tough, tendon-like protein fibres that radiated from the arm and wrist.

The pterosaur's body was covered in hair – or by fibres that looked like hair – and had a mane of longer hair on the back of its neck. This would have helped retain body heat, indicating that it was warm-blooded.

FAST FACTS

FOSSIL FINDS: Britain, France, and Germany

DIET: Mainly a fish-eater

NAME MEANS:
"wing finger"
DATE: 155–145 mya

TRIASSIC	JURASSIC	CRETACEOUS
251 MYA	199 · 145	65 MYA

WINGSPAN: 60 cm (24 in)

Beach hunter

Pterodactylus was superbly adapted for flight. But its big feet and other features indicate that it was a wader that hunted on beaches and in shallow lagoons. Fossil pterosaur trackways found in the 1990s show that it supported its weight on both its webbed feet and the hands at the bend of each wing, with its outer wings folded neatly upwards.

The legs were long and slim, each with four clawed toes. The best fossils have traces indicating that the feet were webbed, like those of a pelican.

Hunter and scavenger

The sharp, pointed teeth of *Compsognathus* indicate that it hunted small animals, and the first specimen ever found included the remains of a lizard in the stomach area of the fossil. Yet, like most hunters, *Compsognathus* would have almost certainly scavenged meat from the carcasses of animals killed by more powerful predators. It would have behaved like a jackal or crow, watching and waiting for any opportunity to snatch a free meal.

The slim, pointed, lightly built skull and jaw were typical of a creature that mainly preyed on small animals such as insects and lizards. Its pointed teeth were very sharp but did not have to be particularly strong.

Compsognathus

The word "dinosaur" conjures up images of colossal long-necked sauropods and predatory monsters like *Tyrannosaurus rex*. Yet many of the dinosaurs living at any one time were much smaller. *Compsognathus* is one of the smallest found so far – a slender, nimble theropod that was not much bigger than a chicken. It would have lived as many birds do now, chasing small prey and picking at scraps, such as the remains of dead animals.

Deadly relations
This lightweight hunter is one of the advanced theropods known as the coelurosaurs, which appeared in the Jurassic at roughly the same time as powerful carnosaurs like *Allosaurus*. The coelurosaurs eventually gave rise to some of the most ferocious Mesozoic predators, including athletic dromaeosaurs such as *Deinonychus* and *Velociraptor* and the massively built tyrannosaurs.

Compsognathus had a muscular yet lean, lightweight body, enabling it to accelerate rapidly and outrun small prey. Similar animals found in China were covered with fuzzy insulating protofeathers, and it is likely that *Compsognathus* had the same furry appearance.

Sharp eyesight would have been vital – both for catching a meal and keeping watch for danger. It might have been a hunter, but it was also prey.

Most of this animal's length is accounted for by its long tail, which provided balance when it was running fast.

Its long, yet slim legs enabled *Compsognathus* to run fast and pounce on fleeing prey. Its arms were relatively short but powerful, with big, strongly clawed thumbs for seizing its victims.

Like other theropods, it ran on the tips of three toes. A fourth backward-pointing toe was reduced to a stump.

FOSSIL FINDS: Germany and France

DIET: Carnivore

FAST FACTS

NAME MEANS: "pretty jaw"
DATE: 151–145 mya

TRIASSIC	JURASSIC	CRETACEOUS
251 MYA	199	145	65 MYA

LENGTH: 1 m (3 ft)

Sauropelta

This impressively spiked and plated creature was an ankylosaur – one of a group of bulky, heavily armoured ornithischians that flourished until the very end of the Mesozoic era. Its armour was mostly defensive, for protection against fierce but quite lightly built predators such as *Deinonychus*. Yet its extravagance suggests that it had some social value, with bigger spikes giving an animal an advantage over its rivals.

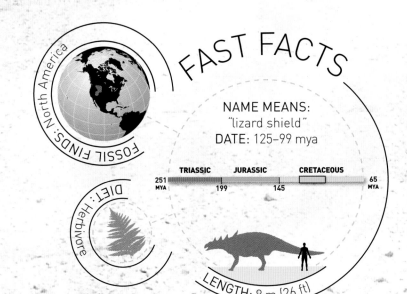

FAST FACTS

FOSSIL FINDS: North America

DIET: Herbivore

NAME MEANS:
"lizard shield"
DATE: 125–99 mya

TRIASSIC	JURASSIC	CRETACEOUS	
251 MYA	199	145	65 MYA

LENGTH: 8 m (26 ft)

Rows of big, bony, tooth-breaking studs extended down the animal's back and tail, and the skin between the studs was reinforced with small bony nodules.

Heavy weapon
There were two main types of ankylosaurs. *Sauropelta* was one of a group called the nodosaurids, which had very spiny armour, particularly on their shoulders. The others – known as the ankylosaurids – were armed with very heavy clubs on the ends of their tails, which were stiffened to support the weight.

The long tail was fringed with blade-like plates that might have made very effective weapons when *Sauropelta* swept its tail from side to side. They could have done a predator a lot of damage.

The most imposing features of this animal were its immensely long neck spines. These had some protective value, but their dramatic appearance must have been just as important, making their weight worth carrying.

Effective deterrent
Although *Sauropelta* lived at the same time and place as *Deinonychus*, their remains have never been found together. By contrast, *Deinonychus* skeletons have been discovered near those of other herbivores. This may mean that the tooth-breaking armour did its job well, encouraging hunters to target less well-defended prey. Since later ankylosaurs evolved even heavier armour, it must have had some survival value.

Second thoughts
Some skeletons of *Sauropelta* have much of the armour intact, so we know how it fitted together. But the shoulder spikes were detached, and early reconstructions showed a single row of spikes on each side. Skeletal clues indicate that there were actually two rows, but we may never be sure unless a skeleton is found with the spikes in place.

Like all ankylosaurs, *Sauropelta* had relatively short, stocky legs and walked on all fours. Weighed down by its armour, it would have been a lumbering, low-feeding animal, rather like a modern rhinoceros.

The broad, bulky body had plenty of room for a big digestive system. *Sauropelta* would have needed this to extract enough nutrients from its tough plant food.

Sauropelta had a beak at the tip of its snout for gathering low-growing foliage, which it mashed up with its many small leaf-shaped teeth. Its mouth was narrow, indicating that it was a selective feeder that chose the most nutritious leaves.

Deinonychus

This fast, agile hunter was one of the dromaeosaurids, the most predatory of the advanced theropods known as maniraptorans, or "hand grabbers". It certainly had big, powerful hands with fearsome claws. More famously, each foot was equipped with a very large curved claw on the second toe, which could be flipped up off the ground to keep it sharp. This sickle claw was almost certainly its main weapon, used for, stabbing or ripping into its prey.

The animal had big eyes that would have faced well forward to give it a degree of binocular vision – essential for an active hunter that needed to target prey accurately.

The teeth were typical of many meat-eaters, being curved serrated blades that would have been very effective at slicing through skin and flesh, but not through bone. Powerful jaw muscles would have given the animal a fearsome bite.

Like many theropods, *Deinonychus* had a slender, mobile, almost bird-like neck, giving its head a wide range of movement. Its body was probably covered with hair-like feathers for insulation.

Breakthrough study
In the late 1960s, dinosaur expert John Ostrom made a study of *Deinonychus* that convinced him that it was a fast, agile, relatively intelligent predator, and almost certainly warm-blooded. This triggered a debate about dinosaur physiology that has still not been resolved, although most scientists now agree with Ostrom. So *Deinonychus* all but destroyed the traditional image of dinosaurs as slow, stupid, cold-blooded reptiles.

FAST FACTS

NAME MEANS: "false lizard"
DATE: 125–112 mya

TRIASSIC 251 MYA · 199 · JURASSIC 145 · CRETACEOUS 65 MYA

FOSSIL FINDS: North America

DIET: Carnivore

LENGTH: 4 m (13 ft)

The long tail may have had a fan of broad-vaned feathers at the end. It was held stiff and straight to balance the animal when it was on the move.

Pack hunter

On one fossil site several *Deinonychus* skeletons were found scattered around a single *Tenontosaurus* (see page 66). This suggests that *Deinonychus* hunted in packs, although it is not likely that it used such sophisticated tactics as modern wolves or lions.

The arms were long and strong, each with three big fingers equipped with stout, sharply curved claws. *Deinonychus* would have used these to cling to its prey when it launched an attack. Feathers on the forearms may have been useful when brooding eggs or young.

The enormous "killer claw" would have ripped into prey like a can opener, inflicting terrible wounds to weaken the victim.

Spinosaurus

This spectacular predator was one of the biggest hunters of all time. It was longer than a tyrannosaur, and probably heavier. Yet despite this, it seems to have been specialized for eating fish, because its fearsome teeth and jaws were just like those of modern fish-eating crocodiles. There were several similar species, all with the same crocodile jaws. Its size was enhanced by long bones extending up from its spine, which may have supported a tall dorsal crest, or "sail".

The weight of the long tail balanced the head and forelimbs, enabling *Spinosaurus* to walk on its hind legs. As with all the advanced theropods known as tetanurans, it had a stiff tail tip.

Sail or hump?
The mystery about *Spinosaurus* is the true purpose of its dorsal crest. Some scientists think that the bones supported a fatty, energy-storing hump, but the weight of this would have been a problem for an animal that stood on its hind legs. The tall bones were light, and it is more likely that they supported a flat "sail" that enhanced the animal's territorial displays. It may also have acted as a radiator, helping *Spinosaurus* lose heat in hot weather.

Long, powerful hind limbs supported the immense weight of the animal's body and allowed it to wade into deep water to hunt fish. It stood on the tips of three forward-facing toes, just like other theropods, and despite its size, it was probably agile.

The very powerful arms had three fingers with huge curved claws, ideal for hooking big fish out of the water.

The "sail" on the animal's back was supported by bones that, at their tallest, were up to 1.8 m (6 ft) long. They were extensions of the vertebrae, known as neural spines. All dinosaurs had these, but they were usually much shorter.

The remains of fish up to 3 m (10 ft) long have been found in rocks that contain spinosaur fossils.

The slender snout bristled with conical, pointed teeth. The longest sprouted from the tip of the lower jaw and interlocked with the upper teeth, just like those of a crocodile. These long crocodile jaws were ideal for plunging into the water to seize fish.

Prey

Spinosaurus was a very powerful predator, and there is evidence that it would have eaten other animals as well as fish. The skeleton of a similar spinosaur called *Baryonyx* was found with the partly digested remains of a small dinosaur in its stomach.

FAST FACTS

FOSSIL FINDS: North Africa

NAME MEANS: "spine lizard"
DATE: 125–99 mya

DIET: Mainly a fish-eater

	TRIASSIC	JURASSIC	CRETACEOUS	
251 MYA		199	145	65 MYA

LENGTH: 16 m (52 ft)

Therizinosaurus

This spectacular animal is one of the strangest dinosaurs ever found. Its bones show that it was an early maniraptoran – a relative of the highly predatory *Deinonychus* and *Velociraptor*. Yet its teeth and digestive system were those of a herbivore, so it seems to have been a plant-eating theropod. Despite this, it was well able to protect itself, thanks to the astonishingly long, sharp claws on its hands, and even tyrannosaurids like this *Tarbosaurus* would have found it a dangerous target.

Instead of the blade-like teeth of a hunter, *Therizinosaurus* had small leaf-shaped teeth for chewing leaves. It even had a beak at its jaw tips, very like that of a plant-eating ornithischian.

Treetop browser

The fossils of *Therizinosaurus* and some of its relatives have been found in southern Mongolia, in part of what is now the cold, arid Gobi Desert. During the Late Cretaceous, this region was warmer and wetter, and there is evidence of tall trees. This fits in with the animal's anatomy, since its immense height was almost certainly an adaption for gathering leaves like a giraffe.

Therizinosaurus had a small, slender head and an elongated neck that allowed it to reach way up into the treetops to gather leaves and other plant food. There were other therizinosauroids, but this is the biggest found so far.

Social calls

If *Parasaurolophus* and its relatives were able to make trumpeting calls, they must have been highly social animals. It is also likely that they lived in dense forests, because sound is the best way of keeping in touch among thick vegetation. Despite this, they probably performed visual displays as well, enhanced by their imposing crests.

Parasaurolophus was one of the bulkiest of the lambeosaurines. Compared to its relatives, it had very chunky limbs and massive shoulder and hip bones. It also had tall neural spine bones extending upwards from its backbone, and these increased the height of its back.

As a maniraptoran, *Therizinosaurus* had long arms that were probably adorned with colourful feathers. It may have used these to keep its young warm at night.

The most amazing features of this animal were its colossal claws. The longest claw bones measure 71 cm (28 in), and each would have been covered with a horny sheath up to half as long again. They would have been lethally effective weapons.

The body was much bulkier than that of a typical theropod. This is because it had to accommodate the big digestive system that it needed to process tough, high-fibre plant material. Despite this, it stood on its hind legs, just like any meat-eating theropod.

Plant-eating theropods

With their small heads, long necks, and big bellies, the therizinosauroids were some of the least typical theropods. Oddest of all is the way they seem to have been adapted to eat plant material instead of meat. In some ways, they resembled the modern giant panda, which is a very specialized type of bear and therefore technically a carnivore. However, the panda has evolved various physical adaptations that enable it to feed almost entirely on bamboo.

Tarbosaurus, a tyrannosaurid that lived at the same time in what is now central Asia, was *Therizinosaurus*'s most dangerous enemy. Like *Tyrannosaurus* itself, *Tarbosaurus* was a massively powerful predator with huge jaws.

FAST FACTS

NAME MEANS: "scythe lizard"

DATE: 83–70 mya

TRIASSIC | JURASSIC | CRETACEOUS

251 MYA | 199 | 145 | 65 MYA

LENGTH: 8–11 m (26–36 ft)

FOSSIL FINDS: Mongolia and Kazakhstan

DIET: Herbivore

FAST FACTS

NAME MEANS:
"near Saurolophus"

North America

Parasaurolophus

The hadrosaurs were the most advanced and successful of the plant-eating ornithopods, with very efficient chewing teeth for

Triceratops

One of the most well-known dinosaurs, *Triceratops* was the biggest of the ceratopsians – the frilled and horned herbivores that were so successful in the Late Cretaceous. Although less flamboyant than some, it made up for this with its sheer size. It was also one of the last of the Mesozoic giants, surviving until the great extinction that ended the era.

Rivers and plains
The remains of *Triceratops* have been found only in the eastern foothills of the Rocky Mountains in North America. In the Late Cretaceous, this region was a wooded plain, drained by rivers flowing into a sea covering the centre of the continent.

FAST FACTS

North America

FOSSIL FINDS:

DIET: Herbivore

NAME MEANS:
"three-horned face"
DATE: 70–65 mya

TRIASSIC	JURASSIC	CRETACEOUS	
251 MYA	199	145	65 MYA

LENGTH: 9 m (30 ft)

The size of an elephant, and with a massive neck shield of solid bone, this animal stood on all four feet and fed close to the ground. Its legs were strongly built to support its weight.

Defence or display?
Triceratops would have been at risk from the giant tyrannosaurs that lived at the same time, so it is likely that its horns and stout neck frill were partly defensive. The animals also seem to have lived in herds for mutual defence. Yet its headgear was very impressive, so it is equally likely that it was used to settle disputes within the herd, such as between rival males.

Many ceratopsians had large holes in the bones supporting their neck frills, but the frill of *Triceratops* was solid. It was bordered by small bony knobs, but did not have many other ornaments.

Triceratops gets its name from the three long horns on its head – the two long brow horns extended to a magnificent 1.2 m (4 ft) or more.

The horny, toothless beak at the front of the animal's snout was ideal for gathering leaves, and its closely packed cheek teeth sheared against each other like scissors to slice up each mouthful. As with all dinosaurs, the teeth were replaced as they wore out.

Fossilized skin fragments show that *Triceratops* was covered with non-overlapping scales, which would have protected it from cuts and grazes.

Eggs and young

Although Mesozoic marine reptiles gave birth to live young, all dinosaurs and pterosaurs laid eggs. Some seemed to leave the eggs to develop untended, like many modern reptiles. But others definitely looked after them just as birds do – incubating the eggs in a nest and brooding the young with their body heat. Some dinosaurs formed breeding colonies, and there is evidence that they fed and defended their young for several months.

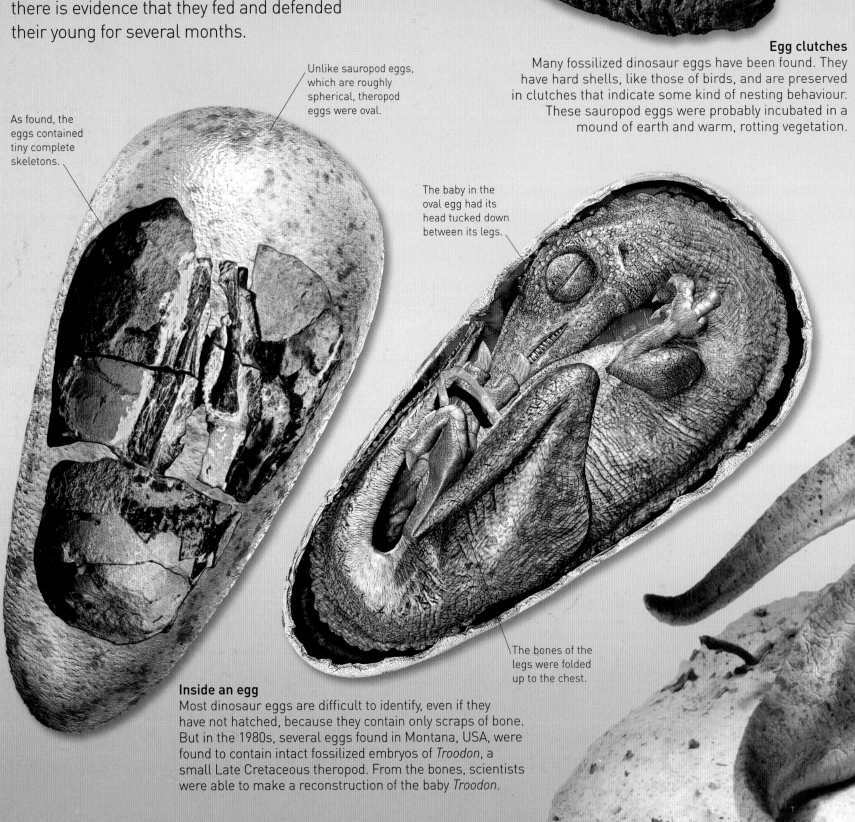

Egg clutches
Many fossilized dinosaur eggs have been found. They have hard shells, like those of birds, and are preserved in clutches that indicate some kind of nesting behaviour. These sauropod eggs were probably incubated in a mound of earth and warm, rotting vegetation.

Unlike sauropod eggs, which are roughly spherical, theropod eggs were oval.

As found, the eggs contained tiny complete skeletons.

The baby in the oval egg had its head tucked down between its legs.

The bones of the legs were folded up to the chest.

Inside an egg
Most dinosaur eggs are difficult to identify, even if they have not hatched, because they contain only scraps of bone. But in the 1980s, several eggs found in Montana, USA, were found to contain intact fossilized embryos of *Troodon*, a small Late Cretaceous theropod. From the bones, scientists were able to make a reconstruction of the baby *Troodon*.

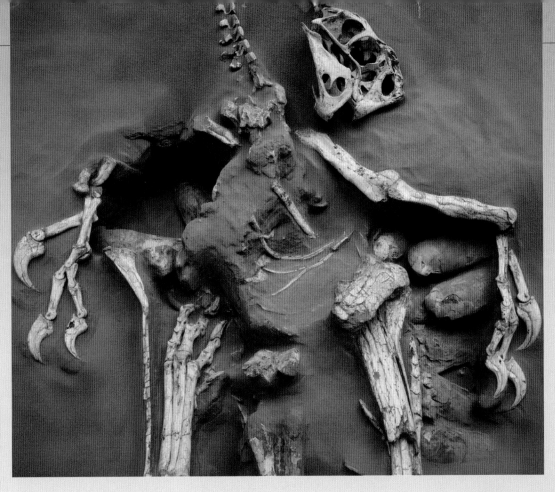

Incubation

In the early 1990s, a site in the Gobi Desert yielded a skeleton of *Citipati* (see page 72) in the act of incubating a nest of 22 eggs. Its long, almost certainly feathered arms were spread over the eggs to keep them warm, as you can see from this fossil. Related animals such as *Deinonychus* (see page 64) have also been found in close contact with eggs. So it seems that many smaller, lighter feathered dinosaurs incubated their eggs like birds.

Nesting colonies

Some dinosaurs nested together in groups. In the 1970s, the remains of a whole colony were found in Montana, USA. The nests were closely packed together, as in modern seabird colonies. Each nest was a mound of earth, with a hollow in the top lined with ferns and twigs and containing up to 25 grapefruit-sized eggs. They belonged to the Late Cretaceous hadrosaur *Maiasaura*, or "good mother lizard".

Growing families

The biggest dinosaur eggs are only the size of footballs, and most are much smaller. This means that dinosaurs grew very fast. The *Maiasaura* young found in Montana were about 46 cm (18 in) long when they hatched, but doubled their size within five months. During this time, they were fed by their parents. After this, they grew faster, reaching about 3.6 m (12 ft) in one year and full adult size of 7 m (23 ft) within seven years.

Maiasaura adults seem to have gathered food for their young.

The infants fed in the nest on leaves and fruit brought by their parents, who also defended them.

Saltasaurus

This big plant-eater was one of a group of sauropods known as the titanosaurs, which appeared in the Late Jurassic and flourished until the end of the Cretaceous. Judging from fragmentary remains, some were truly titanic, with *Argentinosaurus* possibly growing to more than 30 m (100 ft) long. *Saltasaurus* was much smaller, but it is intriguing because its skin was studded with defensive bony plates.

The titanosaurs were the last of a group of sauropods called the macronarians, or "big noses". They had huge nose openings near the tops of their skulls, but these were probably filled by fleshy nasal cavities leading to normal nostrils.

The titanosaur eggs found in Argentina were roughly spherical, and some were found to contain the fossils of baby saltasaurids. When they hatched, these babies would have been tiny compared to their parents, so it is likely that the adults defended them from danger while they were young.

FAST FACTS

FOSSIL FINDS: Argentina

DIET: Herbivore

NAME MEANS:
"lizard from Salta"
DATE: 70–65 mya

TRIASSIC	JURASSIC	CRETACEOUS
251 MYA	199	145	65 MYA

LENGTH: 12 m (39 ft)

Although *Saltasaurus* had the body plan of a typical sauropod, its neck was shorter than many.

Nesting site
In 1997, a vast titanosaur nesting ground was discovered in Patagonia, Argentina. It contained the remains of thousands of eggs, each about 15 cm (6 in) across. It is likely that they were *Saltasaurus* eggs. Several hundred females seem to have dug holes, laid their eggs, and then buried them under earth and vegetation.

We do not know what the teeth of *Saltasaurus* were like, but closely related animals had pencil-shaped teeth adapted for pulling leaves off twigs.

Success story
Until quite recently, scientists thought that the sauropods had all but died out in the Cretaceous. But while these giant plant-eaters may have declined in North America, titanosaurs were a spectacular success in other parts of the world, right up until the end of the Mesozoic.

The body armour consisted of flat scutes of bone and horny keratin embedded in the skin of the neck, back, and tail.

The legs were massive and pillar-like to support the animal's weight. It had stumpy front feet, with no separate toes. Each back foot had five toes.

Quetzalcoatlus

The Late Cretaceous *Quetzalcoatlus* was one of the biggest of the pterosaurs – a giant of the skies with a wingspan of up to 11 m [36 ft]. It could have weighed about 240 kg [530 lb], which is 20 times as much as the heaviest modern flying birds. It is hard to see how it got airborne, and it may have spent much of its time hunting on the ground. Despite this, it was clearly well adapted for both active flight and soaring like a condor.

The very long beak was like that of a huge bird, with no teeth. The animal seems to have gripped its prey with the sharp beak edges before swallowing its meal.

This colossal creature could have easily caught and eaten small dinosaurs like this baby sauropod. It seems to have hunted mainly on the ground rather than flying down and seizing prey from the air.

The neck skeleton was made up of bones that were tightly linked together. So *Quetzalcoatlus* would have had a stiff, straight neck. Despite this, it was able to pick prey off the ground.

Like many of its relatives, known as the azhdarchids, *Quetzalcoatlus* had a big, long-beaked skull topped with an impressive crest. The crest was made of bone sheathed with soft tissue and was probably vividly coloured.

The huge wings were membranes of skin reinforced with tough protein fibres, as in all pterosaurs. They were broad, like those of birds that soar on rising air currents.

FAST FACTS

NAME MEANS:
Named after the Aztec god Quezalcoatl

DATE: 70–65 mya

TRIASSIC	JURASSIC	CRETACEOUS	
251 MYA	199	145	65 MYA

WINGSPAN: 11 m [36 ft]

FOSSIL FINDS: North America

DIET: Carnivore

Death stalker

Scientists used to think that *Quetzalcoatlus* and its giant relatives were fish-eaters. They imagined them soaring over the oceans to snatch fish from the surface. But careful studies of its bones indicate that it was well adapted for walking on dry land, so it is now thought that it soared mainly on warm air currents rising off the land, watching for prey such as small dinosaurs. It would then land to stalk its victims – behaving more like a giant stork than a fish-eating seabird.

As well as supporting the wings, the front limbs were equipped with fingers that were adapted to support the animal's weight. This would have enabled it to walk on all fours, and it almost certainly did this whenever it was on the ground.

When it was foraging on the ground, *Quetzalcoatlus* would have folded its wingtips up and out of the way.

The warm-blooded body would have been covered with fur for insulation. Although heavy by the standards of modern birds, *Quetzalcoatlus* was very light for its size.

Amazing teeth
The teeth were stacked in columns, so as each tooth wore away, it was replaced from below. Altogether, *Edmontosaurus* had more than 1,000 teeth, but only those at the top of each column were in use.

The skull had huge nostril cavities. These may have contained inflatable sacs that made the animal's calls louder.

The big, broad body contained a large digestive system for processing the animal's food. Some of its fossil remains include pine needles, twigs, seeds, and fruit, but we cannot be sure if they were its normal diet.

Edmontosaurus

This very large duck-billed hadrosaur was one of the most successful plant-eaters of the Late Cretaceous, especially in North America. It was highly evolved for gathering and processing vegetation, with hundreds of teeth to grind its tough food to a pulp. In turn, it was the favoured prey of the most powerful land predators that have ever lived.

FAST FACTS

FOSSIL FINDS: North America

DIET: Herbivore

NAME MEANS:
"Edmonton lizard"
DATE: 70–65 mya

	TRIASSIC	JURASSIC	CRETACEOUS	
251 MYA		199	145	65 MYA

LENGTH: 13 m (43 ft)

Edmontosaurus had long jaws that broadened out at the end. They were tipped with a wide, deep beak of horny tissue for harvesting vegetation, which it chewed up with its batteries of cheek teeth.

The back legs were a lot longer and more heavily built than the front ones. But despite this, the animal almost certainly stood on all fours most of the time.

Tyrannosaur prey
Judging from the many skeletons that have been found together, *Edmontosaurus* lived in large herds. As some animals fed, others would use their excellent all-round vision to watch for danger. Even so, many fell prey to hunters. Some skeletons have partly healed injuries that seem to have been inflicted by the teeth of *Tyrannosaurus*.

Its eyes were aimed further forward than those of other theropods. This gave *Tyrannosaurus* better binocular vision so that it could see well in 3-D, judge distances, and target its prey accurately. Studies of its skull indicate that its brain was very well equipped for processing visual data.

Tyrannosaurus

The most famous of all dinosaurs was one of the most formidable carnivores of the entire Mesozoic era. It was a highly specialized heavyweight hunter, with huge, immensely strong teeth and incredibly powerful jaws. They would have given it the ability to kill and eat virtually any animal it ran into. With no serious enemies of any kind, it dominated its habitat as the top predator. So it is not surprising that the only recognized species is called *Tyrannosaurus rex* – the king of the tyrant lizards.

The teeth of most theropods were knife-edged blades, but *Tyrannosaurus* had huge pointed spikes. These were much stronger, enabling it to bite straight through bone. If it broke any teeth, they were soon replaced by new ones.

The arms were tiny, with just two clawed fingers on each hand. They were too short to reach the animal's mouth or even touch each other, and could not have been much help while hunting.

Lethal bite

The extremely powerful jaws and sharp, stout teeth of *Tyrannosaurus* were adapted for biting straight through flesh and bone to inflict terrible injuries. This was almost certainly its main tactic – charging in and taking a huge bite that would either cripple its prey or make it die from shock or massive blood loss. It would then rip its victim apart, gulping down great chunks of meat and even bone.

Tyrannosaurus stood with its body roughly horizontal and its long, heavy tail held out stiffly to balance its head and body at the hips. This stance made it very agile for its size.

FOSSIL FINDS: North America

DIET: Carnivore

FAST FACTS

NAME MEANS:
"tyrant lizard"
DATE: 70–65 mya

TRIASSIC	JURASSIC	CRETACEOUS	
251 MYA	199	145	65 MYA

LENGTH: 12 m (39 ft)

The long hind legs had massively muscled thighs, but relatively slender ankles and feet. This is typical of a fast-moving animal, so it is likely that *Tyrannosaurus* could run very fast.

This *Triceratops* would have been typical prey. *Triceratops* bones have been found with deep holes and scratches that exactly match the size and spacing of *Tyrannosaurus* teeth.

End of an era

Tyrannosaurus was one of several very similar tyrannosaurids that preyed on the plant-eaters of the Late Cretaceous. They all had the same basic build, with tiny arms but massive skulls and teeth. Yet *Tyrannosaurus* itself was the biggest. It was also one of the last – a victim of the mass extinction that ended the Mesozoic era 65 million years ago, eliminating the most spectacular animals that have ever walked on Earth.

Glossary

AMMONITE A marine mollusc with a coiled shell and octopus-like tentacles that was common in the Mesozoic era.

AMPHIBIAN A vertebrate animal such as a frog that usually starts life in water as a tadpole, but turns into an air-breathing adult that lives at least partly on land.

ANKYLOSAUR One of the main types of ornithischian dinosaur, with a body that was covered with bony armour.

ARCHOSAUR A group of reptiles that includes the crocodilians, pterosaurs, dinosaurs, and birds.

ARID Describes a very dry climate or place.

ASTEROID A large rocky object in orbit around the Sun – bigger than a meteor but smaller than a planet.

BACTERIA Microscopic organisms with a simple single-celled structure. Some types live in the digestive systems of animals.

BINOCULAR VISION Seeing a scene or object with two eyes. This enables an animal to see in depth, or 3-D.

BIRD A feathered dinosaur that is able to fly, or is descended from flying ancestors.

BREASTBONE The bone in the middle of the chest, which is enlarged in birds.

BREEDING Males and females coming together to produce eggs and/or young.

BREEDING COLONIES Large groups of animals that gather to breed in one place, usually for mutual defence.

BROODING Keeping young animals warm using body heat and feathers. Sometimes used to describe keeping eggs warm.

BROWSE To feed on leaves gathered from trees or bushes.

CAMOUFLAGE A disguise that helps an animal to blend in with its surroundings.

CANINES The long, pointed teeth of meat-eating mammals such as dogs and cats.

CARNIVORE Any animal that specializes in eating meat.

CARNOSAUR A type of large, powerful meat-eating theropod that appeared in the Jurassic period.

CARRION Meat obtained from the remains of dead animals.

CARTILAGE The flexible gristle that forms the non-bony parts of an animal's skeleton.

CENOZOIC Literally "new animal life", the era of time that followed the age of dinosaurs (the Mesozoic). It began 65 million years ago and extends up to the present.

CERATOPSIAN A horned dinosaur with a large neck frill, such as *Triceratops*.

CHEEK TEETH The teeth in the sides of the mouth that plant-eaters use for chewing their food. Meat-eaters rarely chew.

CLUBMOSS A primitive plant with scale-like leaves and spores instead of seeds.

COELUROSAUR An advanced type of theropod that includes the tyrannosaurids and maniraptorans.

COLD-BLOODED Refers to a type of animal that relies on the temperature of its surroundings to warm its body enough for it to become active.

CONIFER A plant – usually a tall tree such as a pine – that carries its seeds in scaly cones.

CONTOUR FEATHERS The small, stiff feathers that cover a bird's body and help protect it from damage.

COPROLITES Fossilized animal droppings that often contain food fragments.

COURTSHIP Behaviour designed to encourage mating, often involving calling and displays of fine plumage.

CRANIUM The domed top of the skull enclosing the brain.

CRETACEOUS The third period of the Mesozoic era, or "age of dinosaurs", which began 145 million years ago and ended 65 million years ago.

CROCODILIANS Modern crocodiles and alligators and their close fossil relatives.

CROCODYLOMORPHS The archosaur group that includes the crocodilians and similar animals that lived in the Mesozoic.

CRUROTARSAN A major archosaur group that includes the crocodylomorphs as well as various other groups, but not dinosaurs or pterosaurs. Most crurotarsan groups were unique to the Triassic.

CYCAD A tropical or subtropical plant that bears its seeds in large cones, but has a crown of foliage like a tree fern or palm.

DIGESTION The breakdown of food into simpler substances that can be absorbed and used by an animal's body.

DIGITIGRADE Walking or standing on the toes rather than on the sole of the foot.

DINOSAUR One of a large, successful group of reptiles that supported their weight off the ground and probably had a warm-blooded physiology.

DIPLODOCID A member of the dinosaur family that included the giant long-necked sauropod *Diplodocus*.

DISPLAY In animals, a demonstration of fitness or strength, usually designed to impress a rival or potential mate. Some displays can be designed to discourage or distract possible predators.

DOWN FEATHERS Soft, fluffy feathers that, in birds, are purely to keep them warm.

DROMAEOSAUR A type of theropod dinosaur with long, clawed arms and a specialized "killer claw" on each foot. They include *Deinonychus* and *Velociraptor*.

EROSION Wearing away, usually by natural forces such as frost or rain, or waves on the seashore.

EXTINCT Having died out completely and permanently. An extinct species has no living individuals and is gone forever.

FERMENTATION A process in which food or similar material is broken down into simpler substances without involving air.

FILAMENTS Thin, hair-like structures.

FLASH FLOOD A flood that rises very quickly after a rainstorm and may form a powerful torrent.

FLIGHT FEATHERS The long, stiff feathers that grow from the back of a bird's wing and form most of its area.

FLIGHT MUSCLES The big breast muscles that power the wings of a bird or pterosaur.

FOSSIL The remains or traces of any living thing that survive the normal processes of decay or destruction and that are often preserved by being turned to stone.

CYCAD A tropical or subtropical plant that bears its seeds in large cones, but has a crown of foliage like a tree fern or palm.

GINKGO One of a group of non-flowering plants that grows into a tall tree with more or less triangular leaves.

GIZZARD A thick-walled part of the digestive system of some animals in which food is mashed up by muscular action.

HABITAT The environment in which an animal (or any living thing) lives.

HADROSAUR An advanced type of ornithopod dinosaur with a duck-like bill and batteries of chewing teeth.

HERBIVORE An animal that eats plants.

HORNY Made of keratin, the substance that forms the outer layers of animal horns, bird beaks, claws, fingernails, scales, and hair.

HORSETAIL A primitive type of plant that produces spores instead of seeds, and has thread-like leaves that grow from the stem in rings or whorls.

ICHTHYOSAUR One of a group of dolphin-like marine reptiles that was very common in the early Mesozoic era.

IGUANODONT An advanced ornithopod dinosaur with a toothless beak at the front of its jaws, but chewing teeth at the back.

INCUBATE To keep eggs warm so that they develop and hatch.

INSULATION In animals, anything that helps stop heat escaping from the body, such as fat, fur, or feathers.

INVERTEBRATE An animal without a vertebral column (backbone).

IRIDESCENT The glittering rainbow effect created by the way the microscopic structure of an object such as a feather reflects and scatters light.

JURASSIC The second period of the Mesozoic era, or "age of dinosaurs", which began 199 million years ago and ended 145 million years ago.

KEELBONE The enlarged, deepened breastbone of a bird that is well adapted for flight. It anchors the large flight muscles.

KERATIN A tough structural protein found in hair, feathers, scales, claws, and horns.

LAGOON An area of shallow water that has been cut off from the sea.

Hunters like *Compsognathus* would also eat dead meat, or **carrion**.

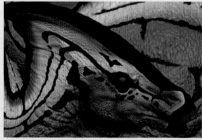

The pterosaur *Pterodactylus* needed big **flight muscles** to get airborne.

Parasaurolophus was an unusually long-crested type of **hadrosaur.**

The Late Cretaceous *Edmontosaurus* was a highly specialized **herbivore**.

MAMMAL One of a group of warm-blooded, often hairy vertebrates that feed their young on milk supplied by the female.

MANIRAPTORAN Literally "hand-grabber" – an advanced type of theropod with powerful arms and claws, which includes birds as well as dromaeosaurs and oviraptorosaurs.

MARGINOCEPHALIAN A major group of ornithischians that consisted of the horned dinosaurs (ceratopsians) and boneheads (pachycephalosaurs).

MEMBRANE A thin, flexible, often elastic sheet of a material such as skin.

MESOZOIC Literally "middle animal life", the era of time that includes the age of dinosaurs. It began 251 million years ago and ended 65 million years ago.

MIGRATION The regular, often yearly return journey that an animal makes in search of feeding areas or breeding sites.

NEOGENE The period of time that forms the second and most recent period of the Cenozoic era. It began 23 million years ago and extends up to the present.

NEURAL SPINES Bony projections that extend upwards from the vertebrae – the bones that form the backbone.

NODOSAURID One of a family of ankylosaurs that did not have a heavy club on the end of its tail.

NUTRIENTS Substances that living things need to build their tissues.

OMNIVORE An animal that has a broad diet, including animal and plant material.

ORNITHISCHIAN A member of the order Ornithischia, one of the two primary types of dinosaurs (the other is the order Saurischia).

ORNITHOPOD One of the three main groups of ornithischian dinosaurs.

OVIRAPTORID One of a family of theropod dinosaurs with beaks and feathered arms, named after *Oviraptor*.

PACHYCEPHALOSAUR A type of ornithischian dinosaur with a very thick skull, including *Pachycephalosaurus*.

PALEOGENE The period of time that formed the first period of the Cenozoic era. It began 65 million years ago and ended 23 million years ago.

PALEOZOIC Literally "ancient animal life", the era of time that preceded the age of dinosaurs (the Mesozoic). It began 542 million years ago and ended 251 million years ago.

PELVIC To do with the pelvis, the skeletal structure that the upper leg bones are attached to at the hips.

PHYSIOLOGY The mechanical, physical, and chemical functions of a living thing.

PLACODONT A turtle-like marine reptile that lived in the Triassic period.

PLESIOSAUR One of a group of typically long-necked marine reptiles with four roughly equal-sized flippers that lived throughout the Mesozoic era.

PLIOSAUR A type of plesiosaur (see above) with a shorter neck, larger head and jaws, and a more predatory lifestyle.

POLLEN Tiny grains produced by flowers to fertilize other flowers so they set seed.

PREDATOR An animal that hunts and kills other animals (prey) for food.

PREY An animal that is killed and eaten by another animal (a predator).

PROSAUROPOD An early, mainly plant-eating saurischian dinosaur, ancestral to the giant long-necked sauropods.

PROTEIN A complex substance that a living thing makes out of simpler nutrients, and uses to form its tissues.

PROTOFEATHERS Hair-like structures evolved by dinosaurs for insulation, which later evolved into recognizable feathers.

PTERODACTYLOID An advanced type of pterosaur (see below) with a short tail, named after *Pterodactylus*.

PTEROSAUR A flying reptile with bat-like wings supported by the bones of a single very elongated finger.

REPTILE A vertebrate animal belonging to the class Reptilia. Modern reptiles are cold-blooded, scaly animals that include snakes, lizards, tortoises, and crocodiles, but warm-blooded pterosaurs and dinosaurs are also classified as reptiles.

SAURISCHIAN A member of the order Saurischia, one of the two primary types of dinosaurs (the other is the order Ornithischia).

SAUROPOD One of a group of giant long-necked, four-footed plant-eating saurischian dinosaurs that appeared in the Late Triassic and survived until the end of the Mesozoic era.

SAUROPODOMORPH One of the two main groups of saurischian dinosaurs, which included the sauropods (see above).

SCAVENGER An animal that lives on the remains of dead animals and other scraps.

SCUTE A tough, often protective plate embedded in the skin, with a bony base and a covering of scaly keratin.

SEDIMENT Solid particles such as sand, silt, or mud that have settled on the seabed or elsewhere. They may harden to form sedimentary rock.

SERRATED Saw-toothed, like a steak knife.

SOARING A form of flight that, over land, involves circling on rising currents of warm air on outspread wings, like a vulture.

SPECIES The basic unit of classification of living organisms. Members of a species look like one another and can reproduce by pairing with one another, but not with members of other species.

SPINOSAUR A type of large, long-snouted theropod dinosaur that had crocodile-like teeth and jaws, adapted for eating fish.

STAMINA The quality needed to stay active for long periods of time instead of short bursts.

STEGOSAUR A type of ornithischian dinosaur with rows of plates and/or spines extending down its back, named after *Stegosaurus*.

STEREO VISION See binocular vision.

SUPERCONTINENT An ancient landmass, such as Pangaea, that is much bigger than any modern continent.

SYNAPSID One of a group of vertebrate animals that includes the mammals and their ancestors.

TEMPERATE A climate that is neither very hot nor very cold.

TENDON A strong, slightly elastic cord-like structure in the body that attaches muscles to bones or bones to each other.

TERRITORY The part of an animal's habitat that it defends from rival animals, usually of its own species.

TETANURAN One of a group of advanced stiff-tailed theropod dinosaurs, which included the carnosaurs, tyrannosaurs, and maniraptorans.

TETRAPOD A four-limbed vertebrate, or any vertebrate with four-limbed ancestors. In practice, all vertebrates except fish.

THERIZINOSAUROID One of a group of plant-eating, large-clawed theropods, named after *Therizinosaurus*.

THEROPOD One of the two main groups of saurischian dinosaurs, which were mainly two-footed meat-eaters.

THYREOPHORAN One of the three main groups of ornithischian dinosaurs, which included the plated stegosaurs and armoured ankylosaurs.

TITANOSAUR A late-evolving type of sauropod dinosaur that survived until the end of the Mesozoic era.

TRIASSIC The first period of the Mesozoic era, or "age of dinosaurs", which began 251 million years ago and ended 199 million years ago.

TYRANNOSAUR A term that is sometimes used for the tyrannosaurids.

TYRANNOSAURID One of a family of coelurosaurs with very short arms and two-fingered hands, named after the big, powerful *Tyrannosaurus*.

TYRANNOSAUROID A theropod that belongs to the same group as the tyrannosaurids and their primitive relatives.

VANE A lightweight sheet of material that responds to air pressure, like a wind vane.

VERTEBRAE The bones that make up the backbone of an animal such as a dinosaur, bird, or mammal.

VERTEBRATE An animal with a vertebral column (backbone) made of a long, flexible chain of vertebrae.

WARM-BLOODED Refers to an animal that uses internal chemical reactions to keep its body constantly warm, no matter whether its surroundings are hot or cold.

The plant-eating *Lesothosaurus* was an early beaked **ornithischian**.

Isanosaurus was one of the earliest four-footed plant-eating **sauropods**.

Coelophysis was a hunter with many knife-like teeth – a typical **theropod**.

The mighty *Tyrannosaurus rex* is the best-known **tyrannosaurid**.

Index

A

Acanthostega 6
air sacs 50, 77
Albertosaurus 10
Allosaurus 50–51
ammonites 31, 61
amphibians 6, 8
ankylosaurs 10, 11, 31,
47, 62–63, 70
Antarctica 31, 40, 41
Apatosaurus 21
Archaeopteryx 54, 56–57
archosaurs 8, 9, 13
Argentina 16, 86–87
Argentinosaurus 86
armour 42, 46–49, 60, 62–63
azhdarchids 88

B

Barosaurus 36, 44–45
Baryonyx 69
beaks 32–33, 88
of hadrosaurs 76–77, 78–79
horny 37, 38, 43, 49, 66,
81, 82
belemnites 31
birds
Archaeopteryx 54, 56–57
brooding posture 73, 84
descended from dinosaurs
6, 8, 10, 30, 54, 72
fish-eating 37
skeletons and features 54–55
success of 61
survivors of extinctions 7
boneheads *see*
pachycephalosaurs
Brachiosaurus 10–11

C

calls 79
Canada 24
carnosaurs 50–51
Caudipteryx 77
Cenozoic era 7
ceratopsians 10, 11, 36, 77,
80–81
China 59, 70, 71, 76
Citipati 72–73, 85
climate 12, 21, 30, 60
Coelophysis 18–19
coelurosaurs 59

colours 76–77
Compsognathus 58–59
Confuciusornis 55
continents 12–13, 30–31
coprolites 37
Corythosaurus 76–77
crests 40–41, 53, 68, 73,
76–79, 88
Cretaceous period 7, 11,
21, 47, 55, 60–93
crocodiles 9, 36, 37, 68
crocodilians 13, 61
crocodylomorphs 31
crurotarsans 6, 8
Cryolophosaurus 40–41

D

Deinonychus 59, 62, 64–65,
66, 67, 85
diet 36–37
dilophosaurids 40
diplodocids 45
dragonflies 13, 31
dromaeosaurids 59, 64–65
duckbills *see* hadrosaurs

E

Edmontonia 70
Edmontosaurus 90–91
egg eaters 72–73
eggs 73, 77, 84–85, 86
Einiosaurus 11
Elasmosaurus 35
Eomaia 61
Eoraptor 16–17, 22
Epidexipteryx 71
Eudimorphodon 26–27
extinctions 7, 31, 60, 93

F

fans 77
feathers 8, 9, 10, 20, 21,
54–57, 64–65, 70–71, 85
protofeathers 59, 70, 72
fish 8, 13, 15, 31, 61
fish-eaters 14–15, 24–25,
26–27, 37, 52–53, 68–69
keratin 42, 48, 52
footprints 28, 53
fossilization 7, 23
eggs 84–85
in limestone 43, 52, 57
mass burials 19, 51

stomach contents and
droppings 37
frills 11, 47, 77, 81
fur 9, 27, 59, 72
see also feathers; hair

G

Gallimimus 71
Gastonia 46–47
Ghost Ranch,
New Mexico 19
Giganotosaurus 61
gizzards 36, 45
Glacialisaurus 40
Gobi Desert 72, 74, 84
Gondwana 30–31
Guanlong 76

H

hadrosaurs 36, 76–77,
78–79, 85, 90–91
hair 21, 53
see also fur
Henodus 13
herbivores 28
Hesperornis 61
Heterodontosaurus 38–39
horns 11, 47
Huayangosaurus 31

I

Ichthyornis 55
ichthyosaurs 8, 15, 24–25,
31, 61
Icthyosaurus 31
Iguanodon 9, 11
insects 13, 31, 61
invertebrates 13, 31, 61
Isanosaurus 28–29

J, K, L

Jeholornis 55
Jurassic period 7, 11, 18,
22, 30–59, 60
Kentrosaurus 11, 46
keratin 42, 48, 52
lambeosaurines 78–79
Laurasia 30–31
Lesothosaurus 32–33
lizards 8, 20, 36, 61
lungs 55

M

macronarians 86
Maiasaura 85
mammals 8, 13, 39, 60, 61
maniraptorans 57, 64–65,
72–75, 77
marginocephalians 10, 11
marine life 13, 31, 60, 61
fish 8, 13, 15, 31, 61
reptiles 9, 14–15, 24–25,
30, 31, 34–35, 84
Mesozoic era 6, 7, 8, 10
Microraptor 55
Mosasaurus 9
Muttaburrasaurus 77
myriapods 31

N, O

nests 84–85, 86–87
neural spines 68–69
nodosaurids 62
North America 24, 47,
51, 66, 80, 84, 85
nostrils 86, 90
Nothosaurus 14–15
ornithischians 10, 11,
32–33, 60, 66–67
armoured 47, 62–63
boneheads 47, 82–83
frills and horns 47
horny beaks 37
spiny 71
teeth 36, 38
ornithopods 10, 11, 31, 76,
77, 78–79
ostriches 20
Ostrom, John 64
oviraptorids 37, 72–73

P

pachycephalosaurs 10, 11,
47, 82–83
Pachycephalosaurus 82–83
Paleozoic era 12, 13
Pangaea 12–13, 30–31
Parasaurolophus 76, 78–79
Pentaceratops 77
Placerias 13
plant life 12, 30, 60
Plateosaurus 22–23
plates 42, 46–49, 70, 86
plesiosaurs 8, 15, 34–35, 61

pliosaurs 34–35
plumes 77
Postosuchus 6
predentary bone 37
prosauropods 22–23
Protarchaeopteryx 54
Protoceratops 37
Protosuchus 31
Psittacosaurus 71
Pterodactylus 9, 52–53
pterosaurs 9, 21, 26–27,
30, 31, 52–53
crests 76
decline 61
giants 61, 88–89
teeth 37

Q, R

Quetzalcoatlus 88–89
reptiles 6, 8
marine 9, 14–15, 24–25,
30, 31, 34–35, 84
warm-blooded 8, 20–21
Rhomaleosaurus 34–35

S

Saltasaurus 86–87
saurischians 10, 17
Sauropelta 62–63
sauropodomorphs 10, 22–23, 29
sauropods 10–11, 28–29, 60, 66
bony studs 47
eggs 84
giant plant-eating 30,
31, 36, 44–45, 86–87
teeth 36
scales 22, 70–71, 81
Scelidosaurus 42–43
scutes 42, 46–47, 70
sharks 37
Shonisaurus 24–25
Sinornithosaurus 21
Sinosauropteryx 70
skulls, thick 82–83
snakes 8, 61
Sphenosuchus 32–33
spiders 13, 31, 61
spines and spikes 45,
46–49, 62–63, 71, 82–83
Spinosaurus 37, 68–69
Stegosaurs 10, 11, 31,
46, 48–49, 60
Stegosaurus 48–49

studs 47, 62
Stygimoloch 47
Styracosaurus 47
synapsids 8

T

Tarbosaurus 74–75
teeth 36–37
of fish-eaters 14–15, 27,
37, 68–69
of meat-eaters 16, 18, 19,
36, 40, 50, 56, 58, 64, 92
of plant-eaters 22, 32,
36, 37, 38, 39, 74, 78,
83, 90–91
Tenontosaurus 65, 66–67
tetanurans 40
Tethys Ocean 13, 14, 30–31,
60–61
Thecodontosaurus 13
Therizinosaurus 74–75
theropods 10, 30, 31, 50–51,
57, 59, 60, 64, 92–93
beaks 37, 43
birds evolved from 30,
54–55
crested 40–41, 76, 77
early 18–19
eggs 84
feathered 21, 70, 71
plant-eating 74–75
teeth 36, 42, 50, 92
toothless 72–73
thyreophorans 10, 11,
42–43, 46, 48–49
titanosaurs 47, 86–87
tortoises 8
Triassic period 6, 7, 9,
12–29, 31
Triceratops 70, 77, 80–81, 93
Troodon 84
Tupandactylus 76
turtles 8
tyrannosaurids 36, 59, 75,
76, 80
Tyrannosaurus rex 10, 60, 92–93

V, W, Y

Velociraptor 10, 36, 59
vertebrates 8
warm-blooded reptiles 8, 20–21
wings 9, 26, 52–53, 56–57, 88–89
young 84–85

Acknowledgements

Dorling Kindersley would like to thank
Stephanie Pliakas for proofreading and
Americanization, Jackie Brind for the index,
and Stefan Podhorodecki for design assistance.

**The publisher would like to thank the
following for their kind permission to reproduce
their photographs:**
(Key: a-above; b-below/bottom;
c-centre; f-far; l-left; r-right; t-top)

5 Corbis: Owen Franken (fcrb/*Citipati* background);
Alan Traeger (crb/*Saltasaurus* background).
6 Dorling Kindersley: Richard Hammond
modelmaker/Oxford University Museum of Natural
History (cb). 6–7 Corbis: Louie Psihoyos (tc). 7
Science Photo Library: Mauricio Anton (bc). 8 Getty
Images: Whit Richardson/Aurora (tr). 9 Dorling
Kindersley: Senckenberg Forschungsinstitut
und Naturmuseum, Frankfurt (tr); Jerry Young
(tl). Getty Images: DAJ (bl/background of
illustration). 10 Dorling Kindersley: Robert L Braun
modelmaker (clb/*Stegosaurus*). 11 Science Photo
Library: Roger Harris (tl). 12 Corbis: Owaki-Kulla
(clb). 12–13 Plate Tectonic and Paleogeographic
Maps by C R Scotese, © 2007, PALEOMAP Project
(www.scotese.com): (c). 13 Dorling Kindersley:
Natural History Museum, London (tl). Getty
Images: De Agostini Picture Library (bl). 14–15
Dorling Kindersley: David Peart (background). 16–
17 Corbis: Jon Spark (background). 18–19 Corbis:
Randall Levensaler Photography/Aurora Photos

(background). 21 Ardea: François Gohier (tl).
Getty Images: Robert Postma (cr). 24–25 Corbis:
Nobuaki Sumida/amanaimages (background).
26–27 Corbis: Mark A Johnson (water and
sky background). 28–29 Corbis: Jon Spark
(desert background). 30 Science Photo Library:
Simon Fraser (clb). 30–31 Plate Tectonic and
Paleogeographic Maps by C R Scotese, © 2007,
PALEOMAP Project (www.sotese.com): (c).
32–33 Corbis: Paul A Souders (background).
34–35 Corbis: Mark A Johnson (background).
36 Dorling Kindersley: American Museum of
Natural History (cra); Luis Rey modelmaker (br).
37 Ardea: Peter J Green (clb). Getty Images: Philip
and Karen Smith (t/background of illustration).
38–39 Corbis: Radius Images (b/fern background);
Kevin Schafer (t/forest background). 40–41 Getty
Images: (background). 42–43 Getty Images: Oliver
Strewe (background). 44–45 Getty Images: Siri
Stafford (background). 47 Bailey Archive, Denver
Museum of Nature & Science: (crb). 48–49 Getty
Images: Holger Spiering (background). 50–51
Corbis: J Joyce/zefa (desert background). 52–53
Getty Images: DAJ (background). 54 The Natural
History Museum, London: Anness Publishing (br).
55 Getty Images: O Louis Mazzatenta/National
Geographic (bl); Spencer Platt (tl). Peter Schouten:
(cra). 56–57 Corbis: Moodboard (background).
58–59 Corbis: Mitsushi Okada/amanaimages
(sky background). 60 Getty Images: TG Stock/Tim
Graham Photo Library (clb). 60–61 Plate Tectonic
and Paleogeographic Maps by C R Scotese,

© 2007, PALEOMAP Project (www.scotese.com):
(c). 61 Carl Buell: (bl). 62–63 Alamy Images:
Eric Nathan (background). 64–65 Getty Images:
Stockbyte (background). 66–67 Corbis: Nick
Rains (background). 68–69 Getty Images: Philip
and Karen Smith (background). 70 Dorling
Kindersley: Peter Minister (bl). StoneCompany.
com, Inc: (tr). 71 Dorling Kindersley: Senckenberg
Forschungsinstitut und Naturmuseum, Frankfurt
(t). The Natural History Museum, London:
Geological Museum of China (bl). Nobumichi
Tamura: (br). 72–73 Corbis: Owen Franken
(background). 77 Mathew J Wedel: (tc). 78–79
Photolibrary: Peter Lilja (background). 80–81
Corbis: Inspirestock (background). 82–83 Corbis:
Radius Images (background). 84 Department
of the Environment, Water, Heritage and the
Arts, Australia: Mark Mohell (tr). Museum of the
Rockies: (bl/fossilized *Troodon* egg). 85 Corbis:
Louie Psihoyos (tl). 86–87 Corbis: Alan Traeger
(background). 88–89 Getty Images: Bob O'Connor
(background). 90–91 Getty Images: Panoramic
Images (background). 92–93 Getty Images:
Willard Clay/Photographer's Choice (background).
94 Corbis: Mitsushi Okada/ amanaimages (fbl/
background of illustration). Getty Images:
DAJ (bl/background of illustration). 95 Corbis:
Randall Levensaler Photography/Aurora Photos
(br/background of illustration); Jon Spark (bl/
background of illustration). Getty Images: Willard
Clay/Photographer's Choice (fbr/background of
illustration).

All other images © Dorling Kindersley
For further information see:
www.dkimages.com

Allosaurus